OVERCOME BURNOUT & ANXIETY,
EASE CHRONIC PAIN,
FIND CLARITY & PURPOSE—
IN LESS THAN 1 MINUTE PER DAY

THE POWER
OF AWE

INTRODUCING THE SCIENTIFICALLY
PROVEN **A.W.E.** METHOD

JAKE EAGLE, LPC, AND DR MICHAEL AMSTER
WITH KAREN CHERNYAEV

First published in the United States in 2023 by Hachette Go,
An imprint of Hachette Book Group.

First published in Great Britain in 2023 by Yellow Kite
An imprint of Hodder & Stoughton
An Hachette UK company

1

A CIP catalogue record for this title is available from the British Library

Trade Paperback ISBN 978 1 399 70806 7
eBook ISBN 978 1 399 70807 4

Printed and bound in Great Britain by Clays Ltd, Elcograf S.p.A.

Hodder & Stoughton policy is to use papers that are natural, renewable and recyclable products and made from wood grown in sustainable forests. The logging and manufacturing processes are expected to conform to the environmental regulations of the country of origin.

Yellow Kite
Hodder & Stoughton Ltd
Carmelite House
50 Victoria Embankment
London EC4Y 0DZ

www.yellowkitebooks.co.uk

PRAISE FOR *THE POWER OF AWE*

"*The* rasting
takes 'quick
boil' hat both
these life-time
benef ing awe at
any r major step
towa: eeded now."

virituality of
ial Healing

"In t duce their
A.W. a of the
COV der. This
origi life and
inspi .

— thor of
A *ur Life*

"*The* ritual
health er of
the w here,
at any ring
but a ies,
and r

id
he

"Eagle and Amster's A.W.E. Method is an extraordinary technique for synthesizing our panoramic understanding of mindfulness, biochemistry, neuroscience, and psychology, and turning it into a pure and conscious laser focus resets the way we feel and opens up our minds to connectivity with others and clarity of thought within. Supported by a boatload of science, the fundamentals of this approach are easily understood and quickly implemented by anyone wanting to enhance their lives. I highly recommend it."

—Rick Foster, best-selling author of *How We Choose to Be Happy*

"This unprecedented work introduces readers to the ingenious practice of micro-dosing on mindfulness. Jake Eagle and Michael Amster are wise and trustworthy guides who explain the science and impact of their research with clarity and confidence. Using relatable examples from clients and their own lives, the authors lead readers through this incredibly simple, yet remarkably profound, technique. *The Power of Awe* is a brilliant book that will revolutionize the way we think about mindfulness."

—Sebene Selassie, writer, teacher, and author of *You Belong: A Call for Connection*

"A brilliant and original take on the emotional state of awe that eloquently illustrates what science is showing: Awe is indeed powerful; it's able to dampen fight–flight responses and activate a parasympathetic state to support calm feelings and relaxation—the only state, we're learning, in which healing of both mental and physical challenges and disruptions can efficiently occur."

—Stephen Porges, PhD, creator of Polyvagal Theory

"*The Power of Awe* is my idea of an antianxiety playbook for parents—and their kids. This simple A.W.E. Method can help turn the tide of our anxiety-ridden society in the most natural of ways—by showing us how to access awe, an emotion that is our birthright and that puts us in a state from which we can better access our resources. The A.W.E. Method is a must-have addition to our antianxiety toolbox."

—Alison Escalante, MD, FAAP, pediatrician, inventor of the Sigh, See, Start parenting method, and adjunct faculty at Rush University's Rush Medical College

"*The Power of Awe* is a breakthrough that integrates the wisdom of all great religious traditions with the insights of modern psychology to bring healing to anyone who seeks it."

—Jack Riemer, rabbi and author of *Finding God in Unexpected Places*

"Safer and possibly more effective than psychotropic drugs, A.W.E. is also more approachable for most of us than meditation. I would argue that the A.W.E. Method offers a simple, free, and effective way to microdose on the biology of love."

—Sue Carter, distinguished university scientist at Indiana University's The Kinsey Institute

"*The Power of Awe* from Michael Amster and Jake Eagle guides us to the vast and miraculous moments of awe in each day and shows us how we can learn to access the healing medicine that surrounds us."

—Christopher Hobbs, PhD, LAc, author of *Medicinal Mushrooms: The Essential Guide*

"In the treasury of diverse meditative disciplines, mindfulness plays an essential role. A.W.E. offers an accessible entry point to begin to explore these realms of extraordinary human potential and reminds us of the transformational potency of small glimpses of well-being accessed many times throughout the day. May reading this book inspire you to continue to explore and discover the vast terrain of profound meditative teachings of which mindful presence is but one core element among many."

—Joel and Michelle Levey, founders of Wisdom at Work and authors of *Mindfulness, Meditation, and Mind Fitness and Living in Balance: A Mindful Guide for Thriving in a Complex World*

"If you've ever been curious about meditation or mindfulness, but not found the time to practice, this book is for you. Bridging the right and left brain—weaving stories and data seamlessly—*The Power of Awe* offers simple steps to improve health and create a well of inner peace. Though I'm usually skeptical of 'three easy steps to . . .' solutions, I trust the research and authenticity of these authors and the immensely useful stories and science that they present."

—Nina Simons, author, speaker, and cofounder of Bioneers

"The A.W.E. Method is the secret ingredient to living a radiant life filled with abundant and divine joy, love, and miracles. In *The Power of Awe*, Eagle and Amster share a novel approach—paired with timeless wisdom—to create your best life now!"

—Sherri Nickols, founder and CEO of The Divine Love Institute and author of *Sexy and Sparkling after 40*

"On every page the authors remind me that I already have a tool inside me to feel better. When I feel awe, even of little things, my perception of circumstances expands, and whatever I am struggling with loses some intensity. *The Power of Awe* is clear and accessible, moving gracefully from firsthand stories of people feeling better in their lives to masterful explanations of the scientific research of awe experiences. This is a manual for understanding our most primitive emotion and should be given to every teenager as a rite of passage into adulthood."

—Sky Nelson-Isaacs, author of *Leap to Wholeness*

"Diving deep into how we construct the world in our minds, *The Power of Awe* challenges us to intentionally cultivate the emotion of awe to quiet the mind's 'monkey chatter' and alleviate anxiety, depression, and loneliness."

—Tor Wager, Diana L. Taylor Distinguished Professor in Neuroscience at Dartmouth College

"Able guides Jake Eagle and Michael Amster empower us to find awe in the ordinary and throughout the day, let go of the filters of naming and categorizing experiences, and open instead to a more receptive state of mind—to reawaken a 'beginner's mind' and take in the breadth of life's majesty."

—Daniel J. Siegel, MD, *New York Times* best-selling author of *IntraConnected: MWe (Me + We) As the Integral of Self, Identity, and Belonging*

"I love this book! It's direct, powerful, heartfelt, and grounded in science. Frankly, I am in awe of the deep practices offered by the authors. A gem."

—Rick Hanson, PhD, senior fellow at UC Berkeley's Great Good Science Center, and *New York Times* best-selling author

"A powerful, practical, science-backed book that shows us how finding awe everywhere, every day is essential to our health and well-being. In *The Power of Awe*, the authors generously share their A.W.E. Method, a novel, and refreshing approach to reduce stress, anxiety, and pain by finding awe in the ordinary."

—Judson Brewer, MD, PhD, *New York Times* best-selling author of *Unwinding Anxiety*

"*The Power of Awe* encapsulates the essence of the healing journey out of chronic mental and physical pain. I have witnessed hundreds of patients break from pain with these concepts. I am in awe of Eagle and Amster's work and how well it is presented."

—David Hanscom, MD, author of *Back in Control: A Surgeon's Roadmap Out of Chronic Pain*

From Jake to Hannah:
Being with you, Being in awe
One and the same
Time stands still, While flying by(e)
Behold the beauty

From Michael:
To my parents, Judy and Harvey Amster, for their endless support
and love that reaches "as high as the sky and as deep as the
ocean blue," and my daughter, Shayna, who has been my greatest
source of love, joy, adventure, and never-ending awe

There are two ways to live: you can live as if nothing is a miracle; you can live as if everything is a miracle. The most beautiful thing we can experience is the mysterious. It is the source of all true art and all science. He to whom this emotion is a stranger, who can no longer pause to wonder and stand rapt in awe, is as good as dead: his eyes are closed.

—*Albert Einstein*

CONTENTS

PART III
A.W.E. AND THE FUTURE OF MINDFULNESS

PART IV
A.W.E. WHEREVER YOU ARE

PART V
DISCOVERING AWE

AUTHORS' NOTE

The stories in this book are true or composites of several cases. In most of the stories, names and other identifying information have been changed to protect anonymity. Any likeness to actual persons, either living or dead, is strictly coincidental.

PREFACE

A SHORTCUT TO TRANSCENDENCE

As lifelong meditators and mindfulness teachers, we confess we were almost embarrassed when we stumbled onto a five- to fifteen-second shortcut to transcendence. This idea ran counter to everything we knew about meditation before we began our research. But, yes, it is possible. It only requires accessing the powerful emotion of awe in ordinary, everyday life. The changes in our lives have been profound, and after seeing the results repeated again and again in our thousands of patients, clients, and study participants, we've proven that our shortcut, coined the A.W.E. Method, works.

A.W.E. stands for Attention, Wait, Exhale and Expand, and the method is a five- to fifteen-second, three-step process—a type of "microdosing mindfulness," or a brief, informal mindfulness practice that also is supported by science. The A.W.E. Method quickly transports us into awe, an incredibly powerful emotion that produces wonderment and a heightened state of consciousness along with some remarkable changes in the mind and body that can improve health and wellness.

Just think about the last time you were in a state of awe—you might have been in the vastness of the Grand Canyon or the Alaskan wilderness, entranced by your favorite performer, or enchanted by the wonder and miracle of life while holding an infant. A smile on your face, or with your mouth slightly open, you may have felt goosebumps or a shiver up your spine. The feeling of awe may have lasted a few seconds or moments. Maybe longer. But no doubt you felt it deeply.

This was not just in your head. During such extraordinary experiences, unbeknownst to you, something incredible was happening inside your body: Your nervous system shifted so that your fight-flight-freeze response became less active while your "rest and digest" functions were more active. In other words, you calmed down and became more patient and less anxious. But you were also energized, entering a kind of playful state. Your proinflammatory interleukin-6 (a type of immune-modulating protein) levels decreased, which if done with enough regularity would reduce chronic inflammation and lower your risk of cardiovascular disease, dementia, diabetes, depression, and much more. Your oxytocin (love hormone) levels rose, increasing your general sense of well-being and your desire to connect.

That is what it means to be in awe—and those effects are just the tip of the iceberg. The still quite young science of awe supports that, when we access the emotion regularly, we experience improved quality of relationships; greater joy, contentment, and life satisfaction; a higher level of cognitive processing; improved well-being and mindfulness; and improved immune function and decreased inflammation. Our research has demonstrated that awe reduces levels of stress, anxiety, depression, loneliness, burnout, and physical pain. Awe also alleviates existential anxiety, a troubled state of mind for which the only other known remedies are religion, medication, denial, and distraction.

It's no wonder that awe has garnered a lot of attention as of late, becoming the focus of dozens of studies beyond our own. According to leading awe researcher Dacher Keltner and coauthor Jonathan Haidt, "Awe-inducing events may be one of the fastest and most powerful methods of personal change and growth."[1]

There is, though, one glaring problem: The average person can't visit the Grand Canyon or see their favorite performer live every day. Unable to access this type of awe daily, people might turn to meditation, a practice that does not require any cost or travel and that has been shown to have many of the benefits previously described. However, we have observed that meditation requires an amount of time, dedication, and effort that effectively discourages far too many people from ever becoming proficient enough to fully experience its benefits. Simply put, meditation is a stumbling block for many people, especially those who can't find even fifteen minutes for themselves in our busy world, let alone thirty minutes to meditate. For those who struggle with silencing their anxious minds—which, ironically, can lead to cycles of negative self-talk as they "fail" to meditate—meditation can become a stressful, rather than a calming, experience.

This is where our research and method come in. In *The Power of Awe*, we offer a clinically proven three-step process to turn ordinary moments into awe-inducing experiences in seconds, giving you a powerful prescription for immediate and expansive personal growth and mental and physical healing. Experiencing awe can happen in as little as five seconds, and it does not require any demanding discipline or skills. Most importantly, whereas many awe studies have relied on researchers either physically bringing subjects to extraordinary places or using virtual reality to simulate that experience, our studies have relied entirely on our subjects finding awe in the ordinary—in their homes, backyards, relationships, and more—opening a new realm of awe research and greater potential benefits for everyone.

Our interest in awe began on a personal level. Jake Eagle, a psychotherapist and mindfulness instructor, had made a career out of helping others reduce emotional suffering, yet he still struggled with never feeling quite satisfied in life. He had what he describes as the "three Hs" (his *h*ealth, his loving wife *H*annah, and a home in a *H*awaiian paradise), and by anyone's estimate, he should have been thrilled to be alive. So he decided to try an experiment, questioning himself every morning: *Am I thrilled to be alive?*

For three weeks, Jake asked himself this question every morning, and he soon found himself actively realizing and focusing on those things in daily life that really were thrilling. This had an impact—he began feeling more positive about his life, even though nothing had "actually" changed. The impact on his life was such that in 2018, Jake began offering a twenty-one-day Thrilled to Be Alive course through Live Conscious, an organization he and Hannah cofounded. The self-reported positive changes the participants shared were remarkable, with one saying, "I feel empowered and like a but-terfly released into a whole new world; observing life from a different point of view and responding to it differently as well."

Through this course, Jake discovered something compelling. He had asked participants to meditate for ten minutes a day to heighten their level of consciousness and get more out of the class, but he soon learned that about half the students weren't meditating because they said they didn't have time. To get around this, he introduced the idea of meditating for a few seconds at a time, and everyone agreed that they could find at least a few seconds in their day to devote to micro-meditations.

Michael Amster, MD, a pain management specialist and mindfulness instructor, happened to be a participant in that course, and he suggested calling these seconds-long meditations "microdosing mindfulness." And the idea caught.

The effects of microdosing mindfulness were completely surprising, even to us. In a survey Jake conducted at the end of the course, the students who did only the micro-meditations reported benefits from the course equal to or greater than those of the participants who were doing more traditional, longer daily meditations.

When Jake reviewed the results of the survey, he was struck that many descriptions people shared reminded him of what he'd read in Michael Pollan's book *How to Change Your Mind: The New Science of Psychedelics*, in which Pollan mentions awe forty times. And the word *awe* resonated for the two of us, who were both going through personally challenging times but felt great emotional and psychological relief through this brief practice.

We were so impressed by the effect of this simplified mindfulness practice that we decided to deconstruct it and figure out what made it so profound. Michael flew to Hawaii so we could spend a week focused solely on this project. We, along with Hannah, reflected upon Pollan's book and the ex-isting research on awe. Working together in the paradise setting of Hawaii, we experienced plenty of dramatic, awe-inducing moments. We determined that getting to awe required focused *attention*, *waiting* in the moment, and breath—specifically *exhaling.* We captured the experience with a fitting acronym: A.W.E.

But then something happened that added an exciting facet to our method. One morning while Michael was doing the ordinary task of making pancakes—something he'd done hundreds of times before—he spontaneously experienced a state of awe. And in that simple moment, it all came together: Microdosing mindfulness (aka, A.W.E.) produced moments of awe, which was remarkable in and of itself. But even more impressive was that A.W.E. produced moments of awe *in the ordinary*—in this case, while watching batter bubble on the stovetop. Now, we were onto something.

MAKING SENSE OF A.W.E.

After that fateful day in Hawaii when Michael reached a state of awe while making pancakes, we were determined to verify and share this profound practice. We each conducted a pilot study. Over a three-week period, Jake taught what we would come to call the "A.W.E. Method" to a group of clients and assessed their mental and emotional health before and after the course. Across the board, participants reported decreased stress and anxiety, feelings of greater connection to others, and increased happiness. Meanwhile, Michael taught the A.W.E. Method to fifteen of his chronic pain patients in a group program, all of whom reported decreased chronic pain, less acute pain flare-ups, decreased anxiety and depression, more connection to others, and greater happiness, gratitude, and generosity.

We could see we were onto something with enormous potential. Michael tracked down Dacher Keltner, PhD, professor of psychology at University of California, Berkeley, and the granddaddy of awe research, to share our results. Dr. Keltner responded with great enthusiasm, saying our A.W.E. Method represented "the future of mindfulness."

We were shocked and honored by Keltner's reaction. Here was this social psychologist and researcher fully immersed in the study of awe telling us we'd stumbled onto something profound. Why did he feel so strongly about A.W.E.? What was he seeing in this informal mindfulness practice? We knew that A.W.E. stood apart from other mindfulness practices because it's so quick and simple. But we needed to confirm that our pilot studies were not just flukes. We needed to test A.W.E. in more than a few dozen people.

Keltner helped us initiate two studies at the University of California, Berkeley. One study tested our method in a sample of more than three hundred patients at NorthBay Medical Center in Fairfield, California, as well as any of their family and friends who wished to participate. The second study involved more than two hundred hospital staff and frontline health-care workers across the United States. Both studies looked at levels of depression and anxiety, loneliness, stress, chronic pain, and well-being. Only the health-care cohort tested A.W.E. against burnout. The studies took place during the height of the COVID-19 pandemic—so the hospital staff and frontline workers in particular were under even more stress than normal.

Meanwhile, we felt the effects of our discovery immediately in our own lives. Shortly after Jake started microdosing mindfulness, at age sixty-five, his outlook changed dramatically. For the first time ever, he felt deeply satisfied in his life. Michael, in his forties, underwent a similar transformation while learning to accept becoming an empty nester. Nothing in our actual life circumstances had changed, only that we had found a way to experience awe regularly—and on command. In all our years as mindfulness instructors and mitigators of human suffering, we had never experienced anything as fast and powerful as the awe that came from microdosing mindfulness.

So, what does it mean to be in awe? We define awe as "an emotional experience in which we sense being in the presence of something that transcends our normal perception of the world." That might sound like a big deal, and it is, but the practice itself is so simple that it can take as little as five to fifteen seconds for a single session. You can try it for yourself right now.

THE A.W.E. METHOD

Attention means focusing your full and undivided attention on something you value, appreciate, or find amazing. Look around the room you're in.

Find that special beautiful something that you value and appreciate. Look at it closely. Really look. If it's a small object, pick it up and begin to notice everything about it. If it's a plant, touch the leaves; notice the texture, color, and smell; and notice the life inside it. If it's a painting, imagine the painter painting it and notice the depth, light, and colors.

Wait means slowing down or pausing. So take a breath—inhale deeply while you appreciate this cherished item in your home.

The final step, **Exhale and Expand**, amplifies whatever sensations you are experiencing. As you exhale—making a slightly deeper exhalation than normal—allow what you are feeling to fill you and grow. What do you notice? Did you smile? Did you relax? Did you feel a warmth in your belly? Did your vision soften, your eyes moisten with gratitude for this precious item you are observing? Did you feel a surge or release of energy?

Congratulations. You have just experienced awe.

PART I

THE SCIENCE

CHAPTER 1

THE SCIENCE OF A.W.E.

On May 31, 2020, news headlines across the country were apocalyptic: "Appeals for Calm as Sprawling Protests Threaten to Spiral Out of Control," "A Mile-Long Line for Free Food in Geneva, One of the World's Richest Cities," "Why We Can't Foresee the Pandemic's Long-Term Effects," "Buildings Around White House Board Up, Protect Valuables Amid Possibility of More Protest Vandalism."

On that same day, amid the chaos and uncertainty of the COVID-19 pandemic, high unemployment, long food-shelf lines, political strife, protests, and racial unrest, we began two robust studies with some of the nation's top awe researchers to test the efficacy of using the A.W.E. Method to ease anxiety and depression, loneliness, burnout, stress, and chronic pain—all issues of mental and physical health. Finding qualified participants was not a problem.

People were stressed more than usual, to be sure, in part because many of us were asked or required to isolate. According to the *New York Times*, in April 2020, just about one month into the pandemic, forty-two states were under stay-at-home advisories or shelter-in-place policies, which affected at least 316 million people in the United States.[1] Holiday and other large gatherings were canceled and friends and families kept apart.

Only essential employees such as health-care professionals, grocery store clerks, and truck drivers were advised to go to work. For many, working at home and connecting with others via videoconferencing became the norm. And so did loneliness. While some grew to like this arrangement, many found the lack of contact with coworkers and the outside world disconcerting.

Millions of others found themselves jobless and facing not only isolation but also financial stressors. With most restaurants and other businesses closed, more than twenty million people were furloughed or laid off during this early stage of the pandemic. That number would only grow.

Meanwhile, health-care professionals were inundated, working long hours covered in masks, gowns, and face shields, watching more patients die alone than usual (the lockdown prevented family from visiting loved ones in hospitals and nursing homes), and under the threat of contracting the coronavirus themselves. Masks were in short supply, even for hospital staff. In many cities, all available ventilators were in use. Vaccines were not yet on the radar, and no one could be certain what the long-terms effects of the virus would be.

AN AWE-INSPIRING VIEW OF THE PANDEMIC

Because of pandemic lockdowns, global carbon dioxide emissions fell by 6.4 percent, or 2.3 billion tons, in 2020. That's about twice as much carbon dioxide as Japan emits every year.

Jackals appeared on the quiet streets of Tel Aviv. Loggerhead turtles laid more eggs on Florida's empty beaches, and endangered river otters showed up in urban areas of Chile. In Llandudno, Wales, wild Kashmiri goats felt safe making extended visits into town, even feasting on hedges.

In Grand Marais, a popular tourist town and outdoor recreation area in northern Minnesota, the silence was

> pronounced. With the lack of local traffic, tourists, and semitrucks from Canada (the border was closed), one resident talked of sitting by a normally busy roadside and soaking up the silence.

Most emerging research is showing that the pandemic made us feel more depressed, anxious, stressed, and lonely. The estimated number of people suffering from mental health issues increased by up to threefold from prepandemic levels. No one, it seemed, was immune. Older adults, those who lived alone, and young adults seemed to suffer the most.[2]

At the time, research about how to best cope with the repercussions of COVID-19 was limited. Our studies, conducted with the University of California, Berkeley, during the early stages of the pandemic when uncertainty reigned, have proven that a regular A.W.E. practice decreases symptoms of depression, anxiety, loneliness, burnout, stress, and chronic pain and improves well-being not only in the general public but also in health-care professionals, even when under more duress than usual.

The studies lasted three weeks. During that time, we observed that the more the study participants dosed awe, the more they benefited health-wise—the more frequent the awe moments, the greater the decrease in negative symptoms, which led to improved well-being. And as participants got in the habit of using the A.W.E. Method over the three-week study period, awe experiences happened not only more frequently but also more spontaneously and often more intensely.

A.W.E. works for more than just overworked health-care providers. A.W.E. works for people with little or no stress and a healthy mental outlook as well. It works regardless of race, sexual orientation, or socioeconomic status (although some research has found that culture and income can influence how likely we are to be open to awe experiences and that awe might be more accessible for people of lower economic status).[3] A.W.E., we learned, works for people who've never tried to meditate. It works for those who've had trouble maintaining a mindfulness practice. And disciplined meditators tend to be surprised at how fast and accessible the A.W.E. Method is.

A.W.E. counters the busy, distressing ways we carry out our lives even when pandemics and riots are not taking place. A.W.E. is a reprieve, a respite from the constant striving we undertake, sometimes just to prove ourselves worthy. Over time, A.W.E. unshackles us from this endless cycle of achievement and self-improvement. We may still achieve and improve but without the endless striving.

A.W.E. is also universal, helping people from different cultures and walks of life and in different circumstances. We'd like to zoom in on Marshiari, a woman who lives in Mexico City among more than nine million other souls. Marshiari joined our study during what was perhaps the loneliest, most intense, and lowest point of her life.

A GLASS OF WATER OVERFLOWING

In her thirties with a two-year-old at home, Marshiari had been diagnosed with an aggressive breast cancer. Her doctors prescribed the highest dose of chemotherapy her body could handle, even though she was allergic to the medication. The horrible side effects, including the threat of going into anaphylactic shock, exacerbated her already intense emotional stress. Marshiari could have used some counseling, but she could only afford treatment at the public oncology hospital, which offered no psychological services.

Depressed, afraid of dying, lamenting that she might soon lose one breast, overwhelmed with all the treatment—and at the same time fearing that the treatment wouldn't work—Marshiari felt not only as if she were losing her physical health but her mind as well.

Such was Marshiari's state when she entered our study to test the effect the A.W.E. Method had on people who were depressed or anxious.

Marshiari signed up for the study because she wanted help—and she trusted the UC Berkeley name. She had no idea what to expect but thought she might have to read or study some PDFs. To her surprise, she was only required to go through "this lovely activity to feel wonder about life." This lovely activity didn't change Marshiari's cancer diagnosis, but it did alter how Marshiari experienced her illness.

> I started to practice A.W.E. during the evenings, when I was lying in my bed, feeling miserable because the chemotherapy was so hard on me. I just looked out the window and paid attention to the beautiful landscape in front of my eyes. I looked at the sky, the *cerros* [hills], or the cows that were grazing on a little hill near my house. I stayed in the moment, forgetting what was going on with my body, and I started breathing in and breathing out.
>
> Within just a few moments, I felt hope and love were part of me. Every time I practiced A.W.E. I had this feeling of gratefulness for every single day I was alive, for my body enduring the treatment and at the same time healing, for the unconditional love of my husband and my child. Sometimes, I felt like crying, feeling guilty I had wasted my time worrying or stressing about events that were out of my control. Something in me was changing. Fear was little, and happiness was growing bigger.

Later that year, in December 2020, Marshiari had a mastectomy, and in April 2021 she officially finished her cancer treatment. At this point, she was looking forward to seeing her friends and celebrating. But the COVID-19 pandemic was still spreading fast. Marshiari got a little depressed, but she kept practicing A.W.E.

> This pandemic has been a nightmare for most of us, but I was able to stay at home without feeling lonely, depressed, or anxious. If I am to be honest, sometimes I feel like a glass of water overflowing . . . but when I practice A.W.E., I just come back to my center and terrifying thoughts go away.[4]

WHAT A DIFFERENCE AN A.W.E. PRACTICE MAKES

It is not an exaggeration to say that the A.W.E. Method changes lives—not what we do or where we live or a medical diagnosis but in how we experience the moments. We have seen these results reflected in our clients, students, patients, and study participants, including Marshiari, who graciously shared her story with us.

Aaron, for instance, gives bigger tips than he used to. He's less frustrated in what can be trying situations, such as delays at the airport. To people he hasn't seen in a while, Aaron appears taller. He attributes this perception to standing with his heart more open and to being more relaxed.

Tom expects to find the silver lining in every situation, even when going to the dentist, which for most of his life he's dreaded. Now he is certain he'll experience something positive, whether it's a nice conversation with the hygienist or a clean bill of health.

When socializing with new people, Olivia is now far less concerned about what others think of her and more interested in connecting with them. She feels more authentic and relaxed in her conversations. As a result, people seem to enjoy her company more.

Michelle has stopped ruminating over things she can't control and no longer finds herself worrying beyond all reason. She feels more resilient. She now feels her emotions with less attachment and more fluidity, which has helped to relieve the physical tension she used to experience frequently in her neck and back. Michelle believes that her closest family members experience her as more available and present.

Angela keeps life in better perspective and feels a connection and beauty to something greater than her life and herself. She has more self-compassion and no longer blames herself for situations of discomfort or difficulty. Her partner has observed that she spends less time feeling bad or guilty about perceived problems. Angela uses a box as a metaphor to describe the effect A.W.E. has had on her life:

Sometimes I find myself trapped in a box created by a story in which I make myself feel regretful and inadequate. To escape the box, first I locate my knowledge of safety: I am healthy, loved, fed, housed, and facing no physical harm. Feeling safe is a kind of stepstool that allows me some stable footing and elevation. Then I remember my A.W.E. practice. Noticing and meditating on something beautiful and transcendental lifts me high enough to peer over the edge of my box. I see beauty and new perspectives. I see choice.[5]

These are real changes experienced by real people who've been using the A.W.E. practice to access awe. Each of them reported experiencing big, effortless, and often spontaneous leaps in personal growth. If you were to take a snapshot of their life before and after A.W.E., you'd see the difference. Perhaps physically—maybe in how relaxed (or tall) they appear—but mostly in how their demeanor has lightened or loosened. Difficulties still arise, but these situations roll off their shoulders more readily. Relationships are easier, and hard conversations are more approachable and less draining.

The changes A.W.E. produces are noticeable and often tangible. We'd like to invite you to try a little experiment. Before you get too far into this book or into using the A.W.E. Method, take a minute to answer the following questions. These are from the Dispositional Positive Emotions Scale, which looks at how naturally prone a person is to experiencing seven positive emotions—joy, contentment, pride, love, compassion, amusement, and awe. Some awe researchers use the awe portion of this scale before beginning their studies to gauge participants' current propensity for awe. We'd like to invite you to do the same. Save your responses, and we'll ask you to repeat this survey again later so you can compare your answers. We think you'll be pleasantly surprised.

DISPOSITIONAL POSITIVE EMOTIONS SCALE—AWE SUBSCALE

Rate how you feel about the statements that follow on a scale of 1 to 7, with 7 being the greatest:

(continues)

(continued)

I often feel awe.

I see beauty all around me.

I feel wonder almost every day.

I often look for patterns in the objects around me.

I have many opportunities to see the beauty of nature.

I seek out experiences that challenge my understanding of the world.

Tally up your points, which should range from 6 to 42. The higher your score, the more you naturally experience awe.[6]

A.W.E. AS AN INTERVENTION

We look at the A.W.E. Method as a medical intervention—a tool we can use to interrupt the course of unwanted thoughts and feelings, shift our nervous system, and ultimately, change our physiology and how we experience any given moment or outcome. We know of no other intervention that will induce states of awe as quickly as the A.W.E. Method.

A.W.E. is a powerful tool for several reasons. First, the method leads us to awe in the ordinary—while cutting into an apple or peeling a banana, for instance. Second, we can find awe in seconds, without booking a flight to one of the Seven Wonders of the World or meditating for ten or more minutes every day. Third, we can call on A.W.E. not only to manage difficult feelings and experiences—as Marshiari and others did during the height of the COVID-19 pandemic when stress, anxiety, and existential dread were at a peak for many people—but also, anytime we want, to feel patience, calmness, and a powerful sense of well-being that ripples throughout our days.

Much research has explored the benefits of mindfulness practices such as meditation and confirmed that they reduce stress and anxiety. Research has also looked at how the emotion of awe serves us, making us less materialistic, more compassionate, and less depressed. As a simple mindfulness practice, A.W.E. gives us the best of both worlds: in only a few seconds' time, and no matter where we are, we can reap the benefits associated with mindfulness practices and awe. This is what our research has demonstrated.

BRINGING AWE INTO THE LAB

Awe is a powerful emotion, associated with the grand, the spectacular, the amazing. So, inspiring awe in a sterile lab setting requires that researchers get creative. First, they must find ways to elicit the emotion in people who are in a controlled environment. Second, they have to figure out how to measure it.

To inspire participants to feel awe, researchers sometimes use virtual reality (VR), a 3D computer-generated simulation that can be experienced through a set of VR goggles or while wearing a VR helmet. If you've ever felt exhilarated (or gotten nauseated) while on a VR ride at Disney World, for example, you understand how real it can feel. VR gives people the sense that they are someplace else, even if the place is imaginary.

Measuring awe in study participants often involves self-report. People are asked to record their feelings of awe in a diary after watching awe-inspiring videos or slideshows, for example, or to determine how likely they are to feel an emotion by filling out the Dispositional Positive Emotions Scale. Sometimes people are asked to recall or imagine an experience of awe to elicit the emotion.

(continues)

(continued)

In some instances, researchers don't tell participants that these exercises are meant to inspire and measure awe. A shift in awe research occurred with the "awe walk," where people were instructed to intentionally look for awe as they walked mindfully in nature.

Other than awe walks, the A.W.E. Method is the only intervention we're aware of that can be used to bring on a full awe experience in the ordinary—even in a lab setting.

For our studies, we relied on self-report in the form of questionnaires and diaries. On Day 0, we asked participants to fill out a forty-five-minute entrance survey that assessed their baseline levels of mental, physical, and emotional health. Over the course of twenty-one days, participants attended four sixty-minute online A.W.E. sessions during which we talked about awe and the A.W.E. Method. We also discussed anxiety, distinguishing between actionable and existential anxiety, and how A.W.E. can be used for both. (We talk about these differences in Chapter 10.) Finally, we discussed force versus presence. A.W.E., in other words, should be easy instead of involving effort, striving, and judging. Because people tend to judge themselves when learning new skills, we encouraged participants not to worry about how their A.W.E. practice was going. Like the Nike ad says, we wanted them to "just do it."

We also asked everyone to practice A.W.E. at least three times each day for about five to fifteen seconds—less than one minute per day—to develop their "A.W.E. muscle." To help everyone in the study remember to practice A.W.E., we supplied wristbands labeled "Attention. Wait. Exhale and Expand." Most people found them useful, at least initially as a reminder. We also invited everyone to share their awe moments on our website (ThePower OfAwe.com), which features a running collection of photographs and words posted by people who use the A.W.E. Method. Throughout the study, many people asked questions—not necessarily about how to microdose awe but usually about their experiences with A.W.E. Mostly, participants were curious about what was happening to them. Every third day, we answered everyone's questions in a summary email.

On all but the first (Day 0) and last (Day 23) days of the study, we asked participants to fill out a five-minute daily diary survey that assessed their current levels of mental, physical, and emotional health as well as their adherence to the A.W.E. intervention. On Day 23, participants completed a forty-five-minute exit survey that was nearly identical to the entrance survey.

Our results neatly reflected what we found in our smaller pilot studies. Through these daily diaries and the entrance and exit surveys, as well as various measures throughout the study, we were able to track statistically significant changes in participants who microdosed awe three times a day for at least five to fifteen seconds. A.W.E. resulted in the following:

- Fewer physical stress symptoms, including pain
- Lower perceived stress
- Fewer depressive symptoms and anxiety symptoms
- Lower perceived loneliness
- Lower perceived burnout
- Overall improvement in feelings of mindfulness and well-being

In a matter of seconds, A.W.E. was achieving the same or better results than many mindfulness practices and other therapeutic interventions that required more time and effort. Here's a closer look at some of our findings.

In the past, I have had years of anxiety, fears, aggression, and an overactive mind. A.W.E. has brought out my childlike curiosity and the joys of seeing, hearing, and smelling life around me. Waking in the morning and hearing the various new bird sounds outside our windows starts my day with calm. I'm in awe so much *just looking out over our terrazzo each day. When I find myself be-coming irritated, I look around at something in my vicinity and in-stantly find joy. My life is more enjoyable, and I'm sure those who know me appreciate that too.*[7]

—Denise

DEPRESSION AND ANXIETY

Depression and anxiety disorders are common and disruptive. In the United States, we've been on a trajectory of increased depression and anxiety since the late 1980s. Worldwide, more people (up to 8 percent of the global prepandemic population and up to 59 percent of the population during the pandemic) suffer from depression and anxiety than any other mental health issue.[8] How much these disorders disturb us ranges from mild to severe.

Although depression and anxiety are mental health issues, they affect us physically as well. Even mild cases of depression and anxiety can alter health and well-being, causing digestive, heart, respiratory, sleep, and thyroid problems.

Current interventions for depression and anxiety include medication, talk therapy, mindfulness, and exercise. These treatments work for some people some of the time. But the bottom line is that there isn't strong enough evidence to say with any certainty whether what we're currently doing to help the millions of people who suffer from depression and anxiety is adequately addressing the problem. For the most part, the research shows that there's much room for improvement.

Treating depression is troublesome in part because the causes range from giving birth to experiencing trauma or loss to having a heart attack. Often, medication is used to treat the depression but not the underlying cause. This may partially explain the findings of a Centers for Disease Control and Prevention survey, which determined that more than 13 percent of adults in the United States take antidepressants to manage depression.[9] Although medication helps many people, there's room for improvement. A more recent study shows that antidepressants don't improve health-related quality of life for most people.[10]

Similarly, a long-term solution for anxiety has eluded medicine and psychology. Cognitive behavioral therapy (CBT), a treatment model that helps patients change unhelpful thinking patterns, and therefore behaviors, has been shown to reduce general anxiety disorder. But, as helpful as therapy can be, it's still a form of striving—we must *try* to be better by thinking up more appropriate responses to what angers or scares us. All this requires ongoing effort.

Antianxiety medications, which include the brand-name drugs Xanax, Klonopin, Valium, and Ativan, work more quickly, but they are not a cure. The medication eventually wears off and the anxiety returns, especially in those who haven't taken other steps to remove sources of anxiety from their lives or learned to deal effectively with those that can't be removed.

Further, some drugs used to treat anxiety, such as benzodiazepines, cause dependency and after consistent repeated use the body develops a tolerance to the drug and its impact wanes. To make up for the decreased effect, the inclination is to take more than prescribed. If this happens, anxiety-ridden individuals may then have the added angst of addiction.

Mindfulness practices have long been known to reduce acute symptoms of depression and, to a lesser extent, anxiety.[11] Mindfulness-based cognitive behavioral therapy (MCBT) shows promising results for preventing relapse into major depressive disorder (MDD).[12] MCBT combines mindfulness with CBT, and the in-person group sessions offer the added benefit of social interaction. We have found A.W.E. to be a convenient option to MCBT and other therapies and an important addition to the storehouse of techniques used to address depression and anxiety.

Through our research, we learned that A.W.E. is a remarkably effective tool that provides relief from depression and anxiety and even accelerates progress in talk therapy, according to some of the study participants. A.W.E. works in part because it targets the source of what ails us—our state of mind—and invites us to see our situation through a new lens.

For our study of the effect of A.W.E. on depression and anxiety, we divided participants into two groups: health-care workers and those from the general population. After three weeks of practicing the A.W.E. Method, both groups experienced a significant improvement, with those from the health-care group showing a 35 percent reduction in depressive symptoms and a 21 percent reduction in anxiety. The general population fared even better, reducing depression by 36 percent and anxiety by 24 percent— impressive results for a practice that's free, harmless, and has an efficacy rate that improves over time. Even more striking is that participants from both groups who reported having mild depression before practicing A.W.E. reported having *no symptoms of depression* afterward.

My anxiety has been pretty high and hard to manage, but when I am walking and I pause and focus on nature's colors, smells, the way the air feels and keep coming back to this, I am reminded of what is here. I lose myself in the colors of leaves and listen to the sounds they make in their familiar seasonal shift. Even when it's really hard to manage anxiety, nature is always my medicine of awe.

Awe is a gift that's always here for us if we keep that space in our mind and heart to let it in as we can. When my partner and I are having a difficult time and my mind gets lost down an anxious path, I refocus on the golden fall leaves, and it reminds me of the seasons and its lessons and nourishment. What is here and what is true no matter the obstacles. I am in awe of the practice of A.W.E.[13]

—Natalie

THE MATRYOSHKA MODEL

Our study results show that A.W.E. works to alleviate symptoms of mild depression, and we believe A.W.E. may even be a viable option for people who have major depressive disorder (MDD).

Recently, researchers at the Catholic University of the Sacred Heart of Milan looked at the emotion of awe as an intervention for MDD. They considered research that shows how awe affects us via four dimensions: psychologically, hormonally, neuropsychologically, and existentially. Combined, these effects produce a sudden change in which we are no longer our same self—we transform. "Awe," they said, "is a complex and transformative emotion that can restructure individuals' mental frames so deeply that it could be considered a therapeutic asset for major mental health issues, including depression."[14]

These researchers framed awe's functions into what they call the Matryoshka Model—each dimension of awe being like a Russian Matryoshka, the painted wooden dolls that nest neatly within one another. The researchers thought the nested structure of the Matryoshka a suitable metaphor for representing the nested structure of the awe experience.[15]

They determined that the awe process begins with neurological changes that involve how brain neurons are firing, followed by psychological changes in how we perceive reality, followed by changes in the endocrine system (release of hormones), followed by existential changes, such as exploring the meaning of life and spiritual well-being.

These researchers also found that the more we experience awe, the more we can sustain the feeling of awe so that it becomes more than a fleeting experience—not just a state but a trait (we talk more about state versus trait in Chapter 11). In other words, awe could effectively alter the course of MDD.

Depression and anxiety have many different sources. Loneliness is a common contributor. And so we looked at whether cultivating the emotion of awe—which is known to increase our sense of belonging, interconnectivity, and collective identity—would help to reduce feelings of loneliness.

LONELINESS

Loneliness is more a state of mind than a state of being. We feel lonely when we *perceive* that we don't feel as connected to others as we'd like to be. If two people were leading parallel lives, but one was content being alone and the other found it distressing, the former might perceive they are happy and the other might perceive they are lonely.

Loneliness is a chronic problem for many Americans: About one in five adults often or always feel lonely. As with depression, loneliness has been on the rise for decades, and we suffer mentally and physically because of it. Chronic loneliness has been associated with sleep disorders, dementia, depression, anxiety, cardiovascular disease, stroke, and more. The heart seems to be affected significantly. A recent study found an elevated risk—from 13 to 27 percent—of cardiovascular disease in postmenopausal women who experienced social isolation and loneliness.[16] Even more concerning is that people who perceive themselves to be lonely have a 50 percent chance of dying prematurely.[17]

We are social beings. Our health depends on feeling connected, yet getting help for loneliness can be difficult and can even feel counterintuitive. As Harvard professor of psychiatric epidemiology Karestan Koenen said, "If you're lonely, almost the last thing you want to do is reach out."[18]

To determine whether using A.W.E. to generate feelings of awe could help assuage feelings of loneliness, we again looked at our two cohorts: healthcare professionals and the general population. Again, this was during the COVID-19 pandemic when interacting with others came to a halt for many of us or, in the case of health-care workers, was stressful.

To guide us in measuring pre- and post-A.W.E. perceptions of loneliness, we asked participants to complete a version of the UCLA Loneliness Scale, answering on a scale of 1 to 4 such questions as "How often do you feel as if no one understands you?" For the twenty-one days of the study, participants used a diary to report their experiences regarding how lonely, connected, and positive they felt.

UCLA LONELINESS SCALE (SHORT FORM)

INSTRUCTIONS
The following statements describe how people sometimes feel. For each statement please indicate how often you feel the way described using the numbers below. There are no right or wrong answers.

1 = NEVER   2 = RARELY   3 = SOMETIMES   4 = ALWAYS

How often do you feel unhappy doing so many things alone?
How often do you feel you have no one to talk to?
How often do you feel you cannot tolerate being so alone?
How often do you feel as if no one understands you?
How often do you find yourself waiting for people to call or write?
How often do you feel completely alone?
How often do you feel unable to reach out and communicate with those around you?
How often do you feel starved for company?
How often do you feel it is difficult for you to make friends?
How often do you feel shut out and excluded by others?

(continues)

(continued)

SCORING
A total score is computed by adding up the response to each question. The average loneliness score on the measure is 20. A score of 25 or higher reflects a high level of loneliness. A score of 30 or higher reflects a very high level of loneliness.

UCLA Loneliness Scale © Dr. Daniel Russell

The more participants felt awe, the more connected they felt. This is a fascinating aspect of awe. Lonely people want companionship. Although awe doesn't offer companionship, it gives us a sense of connection to something greater than ourselves. And it does something else, which we'll delve into in Part II: this internal sense of connection to the world or something greater than ourselves alters our nervous system so we're more available to connect with people in a healthier way. Awe makes us feel whole, and so we enter relationships out of wholeness instead of neediness and others are drawn to us because of that.

A.W.E. gives us some control over our loneliness. Using the A.W.E. Method, we don't need a companion to come and be our friend (although that would be welcome). In awe, we experience a sense of connection that is not dependent on other people.

This sense of connection is an awe trait, and many studies have shown that awe leads to connection by getting us to focus less on self, become more aware of our interconnectedness to others, and even feel a sense of oneness with other people.[19] Relying on this unique trait of awe, A.W.E. reduced loneliness by 12 percent in the general population and 15 percent in health-care workers.

By way of comparison, in a study on loneliness and sleep problems in physicians during COVID-19—a study very similar to ours in terms of population, timing, length, and the use of a mindfulness practice—researchers at WellSpan York Hospital in Pennsylvania asked half of the participants to practice a daily heartfulness meditation for four weeks. In this study, the 155 participants were randomly assigned to the control group or the intervention, which consisted of listening to a six-minute Transcendental Meditation heartfulness relaxation recording in the morning and before sleep. The result was a 7 percent improvement: the physicians who practiced the meditation felt less lonely and slept better.[20] In comparison, our study showed that the A.W.E. Method was more than twice as effective as the heart meditation.

> I am in touch with awe and delight everyday. Awe is magical and can transcend any circumstance. For instance, I was frustrated that my brother was not answering my emails, texts, or phone calls. I felt lonely and wondered whether I had offended him. Then I suddenly recalled that I can re-create my experience. I became deeply aware of my love for him and compassionate about what he is going through. I realized it was not about me at all. I reached out with no expectation, and he called me the next day. We had a wonderful dinner together. A.W.E. is a reminder. It helps me see myself get into my "machinery" and make the choice to give up whatever story I am telling myself that gets me reacting.[21]
>
> —Estelle

We'll cover more about connection and awe in Chapter 3 and elsewhere. But a point we want to highlight is that A.W.E., *even when practiced in isolation*, can produce the sense that we are connected and thereby reduce perceptions of loneliness.

BURNOUT: RAMPANT AND DEADLY

Burnout happens when we are physically and mentally exhausted, usually because we've been stressed or frustrated and functioning on too little sleep. This combination can't last forever. Eventually, like an engine that's been running on fumes, we've no choice but to stop.

Perhaps no other industry experiences as much burnout as health care. This was true before the pandemic, when burnout rates averaged 30–50 percent. During the pandemic, when hospitals and clinics were understaffed and employees were overworked and concerned about catching and spreading the virus to loved ones at home, burnout rates ranged from 40 to 70 percent, with frontline nurses and doctors being some of the hardest hit.[22]

During the period when we were conducting our studies, the American Medical Association surveyed more than twenty thousand physicians and other health-care workers on how they were coping during COVID-19. The degree of burnout was alarming: 43 percent suffered from work overload— for example, working long hours caring for more patients than usual—and 49 percent said they were burned out on the job.[23]

Burnout is not something to take lightly. Mental and physical health take the brunt. Traumatized by the magnitude of what they must confront for long hours every day, frontline health-care workers, for instance, found themselves with thoughts and conditions they'd never before experienced. Symptoms were like those of post-traumatic stress disorder (PTSD) and included an inability to focus, depression, anxiety, thoughts of suicide, exhaustion, and more. Lack of sleep alone can result in conditions as serious as cardiovascular disease and even psychosis.[*] Feeling demoralized, many thought of leaving their profession.[24] And for some, that was the only remedy.

Burnout has serious consequences in any profession. In health care, it can be deadly. In hospitals and clinics, errors resulting from burnout lead to a hundred thousand patient deaths annually.[25] Doctors make more mistakes when stressed and sleep deprived, potentially endangering the lives of patients. Nationally, approximately three hundred physicians commit suicide each year because of depression, a common result of burnout.[26]

---

* Depriving an individual of sleep is a well-known form of torture used in many countries, including the United States. That we allow these conditions in health care and other industries seems appalling when considering the mental and physical health consequences. Even the *Guinness Book of World Records* has removed its entry for the person who's gone the longest time without sleep.

When health-care workers quit their jobs because of burnout, existing staff are overtaxed and more susceptible to burnout, perpetuating an endless cycle of exhaustion. Attracting people to a profession with high burnout rates is difficult at best. The nursing shortage during the pandemic is a prime example: Before the pandemic, about 40 percent of nurses reported burnout. By January 2021, the percentage had grown to 70 percent.[27] Meanwhile, the demand for nurses is growing, as burnout is causing many nurses to retire early. And between 30 and 60 percent of those fresh out of nursing school decide the profession is not for them.[28]

Burnout has been an issue for years, but many interventions for doctor burnout have been shown to be ineffective, even those that use mindfulness practices. We searched the literature, and even eight-week-long mindfulness-based stress reduction programs (MBSRs) were not effective, even though MBSR has been shown to be effective for stress reduction in the workplace. We suspect that part of the reason for this lack of efficacy is that no intervention, no matter how effective, can be a substitute for a good night's sleep. (Anecdotally, some of our study participants found themselves sleeping for longer intervals by practicing the A.W.E. Method before bedtime.)

In looking at the A.W.E. Method and its effect on health-care professionals and burnout, we asked participants to complete the Maslach Burnout Inventory, a list of twenty-two job-related questions, before and after the A.W.E. intervention.[29] After practicing A.W.E. for twenty-one days, burnout symptoms were reduced by 8 percent, which is impressive considering that the magnitude of the pandemic worsened throughout 2020, with no end in sight, and that the mental health of most health-care workers was getting worse, not better.

BURNOUT CAN AFFECT ANYONE

We don't need to be a health-care worker during a pandemic to experience burnout. A prepandemic (2018) Gallup Poll stated that two-thirds of all employees across occupations feel burned out at least some of the time.[30]

Dealing with burnout requires some much-needed self-care—sleep, exercise, recreation, healthy diet, hydration, breaks, and maintaining relationships with friends and family.[31] If burned-out pandemic-era workers were going to take care of themselves, quitting may have seemed like the only option. In what has become known as the Great Resignation, more than thirty-eight million people quit their jobs across all sectors in 2021, a quit rate of 33 percent—a higher percentage of the workforce than in any other year on record.[32] Burnout, along with a shift in personal priorities triggered by the pandemic, was a leading cause of this mass exodus.

The A.W.E. Method has an advantage over other mindfulness interventions for burnout. First, workers can access it at any time while on or off the job and complete the intervention in less than a minute. Second, A.W.E. doesn't require willpower—we don't have to sit for an extended period in silence and hope that the thoughts swirling through our mind eventually go away. Third, A.W.E. has a cumulative effect—awe experiences build on one another, even changing neural pathways in the brain (we'll get to this in Chapter 11). Fourth, A.W.E. pretty much guarantees a reward—we're left feeling delighted, refreshed, and less constricted after just fifteen seconds of practice. The A.W.E. Method can be helpful in alleviating burnout because awe expands our awareness, helping us to perceive what is beyond our stressful situation. And this is helpful because, according to Dacher Keltner, most of us are "awe deprived."[33]

Burnout's partner in crime is stress. When we looked at stress levels in our two cohorts, we again found A.W.E. to be an effective intervention.

STRESS AND WELL-BEING

Every year since 2007, the American Psychological Association (APA) has partnered with the Harris Poll to conduct a survey of stress levels across the United States. During most years, people surveyed report that money, work, and the economy are their biggest stressors, followed by health care, mass shootings, and climate change. That changed in 2020 and 2021. While these leading stressors still existed, they were topped by worries over the pandemic, the future of the United States as a nation, discrimination, and police violence toward marginalized people.* The APA was alarmed: "These compounding stressors are having real consequences on our minds and bodies. . . . We are facing a national mental health crisis that could yield serious health and social consequences for years to come."[34]

Since the pandemic, nearly half of adults have reported that they anger more easily, suffer from unexpected moods swings, and feel increased tension in their bodies. The adults in Gen Z (ages eighteen to twenty-three), faced with an uncertain future, showed higher stress levels than other generations.

When suffering from stress, we're not our best selves. We're short with the people we love, tend to easily lose focus, and have a hard time making decisions. Physical symptoms of stress can include headaches, stomachaches, chronic pain, and skin rashes. Chronic stress is often a gateway to depression and anxiety. Having an existing mental or physical health problem usually worsens stress.

Some people deal with stress by self-medicating—turning to alcohol and other drugs—or distracting themselves by gambling or playing computer games compulsively. Healthier approaches to ease stress include relaxation techniques, such as soaking in a hot bath, stretching, meditating, spending time in nature—and finding awe.

When veterans, at-risk youth, and college students were asked to find awe in nature, their level of well-being rose significantly after just one week.[35] Other studies show that awe increases life satisfaction, at least momentarily, and daily well-being.[36] And awe doesn't just shift the way we think; it changes our biology. According to a 2015 study in the journal *Emotion*, awe, more than any other positive feeling, was linked to lower levels of a molecule called interleukin-6, which is associated with stress and inflammation.[37] (We'll talk more about A.W.E. and biology in Chapter 2.)

---

* Thirty-three percent of adults surveyed felt stress for being discriminated against personally; 59 percent of adults cited discrimination and police violence in general—whether affecting them personally or not—were major stressors.

During the early days of the pandemic, I was stuck in a pattern of staying up late to make sure nothing bad would happen. Out of the blue, a friend sent me a link to a study on the practice of A.W.E. Life had changed into such murky, muddy waters, I believed almost anything was worth looking into. Even if it sounded a bit "foo-foo" to this trained research nerd.

The practice of A.W.E. turned out to be life changing for me. Up to then, I was mostly unwilling to move into a state of living in the moment or take time to appreciate the journey of now.

Learning the practice of finding awe during the pandemic allowed me to make fundamental life changes. For example, I was staying up three to four hours past my typical bedtime playing inane computer games so I could win at something. I think I stayed awake to "assure" personal safety too. In my state of hyperalert, I slept in one-hour intervals. I got irritated with my cats for being cats and let my frustrations with normal cat behavior be evident to them (quarantined, I was mostly alone with them!). I focused on the stressors of the divisive political scene and my pandemic-impacted life. I spent most of my time worrying about things over which I had no control.

After learning A.W.E., I found moments to celebrate personal safety by paying attention to what is rather than what could be and remarkably curtailed my incessant computer game playing. I employed the practice of A.W.E. when I went to bed and increased sleep intervals from three to five hours (a huge deal).

As if that weren't enough, I celebrated differences and paid more attention to the now and what was in my purview. I decided to find the perceptions of others awesome and let go of my need to put my spin on any of it. I accepted where they were and let go of where I was or was not in their story.

For me, finding awe moments in the ordinary has become second nature.[38]

—Sally

Our stress and well-being study looked at emotional, psychological, and social well-being as well as perceived stress levels in our same two groups: health-care professionals and the general population. To determine these levels, we used the Mental Health Continuum Short Form, which asks questions within each of the three domains, and the Perceived Stress Scale, which asks ten questions related to stress levels and then rates perceived levels of stress from low to high depending on the answers.

When looking at whether daily experiences of awe caused daily changes in subjective stress, physical stress (such as headaches and stomachaches), and general well-being, we found that people who reported experiencing higher levels of awe also reported lower levels of subjective stress, lower physical stress, and greater well-being.

In additional analyses, the more the participants experienced awe on a daily basis, the more they experienced long-term well-being. In other words, daily doses of awe during the peak of the COVID-19 pandemic were beneficial for people's physical and psychological health.

The end results were impressive as well: after twenty-one days of practicing A.W.E., both groups showed a significant decrease in stress and stress-related physical symptoms—18 percent for the health-care worker group and 17 percent for the general population group.

CHRONIC PAIN

Chronic pain develops in the months and years following an injury, lasting beyond the expected time of healing. It's different from acute pain, which is temporary and lasts a few days or weeks after a physical injury or surgery. In the United States, upward of fifty million adults suffer from chronic pain—pain that persists beyond what's considered a normal recovery period.[39]

When Michael trained as a pain specialist almost twenty years ago, the prevailing belief was that chronic pain resulted from an anatomical problem in the body and that pain was effectively treated with medications, injections, physical therapy, and sometimes surgery. In the 1990s, innovative leaders in the field of pain management, starting with John Sarno, MD, demonstrated that *most* chronic pain is not due to a structural problem within the body but is a learned phenomenon that occurs in the brain. Dr. Sarno wrote, "Pain syndromes look so 'physical' it is particularly difficult for doctors to consider the possibility that they might be caused by psychological factors, and so they cling to the structural explanation. In doing so, however, they are chiefly responsible for the pain epidemic that now exists in this country."[40] He was very prescient, as the epidemic has grown far worse since he first made that claim in 1991.

More recently, Alan Gordon, author and founder of the Pain Psychology Center, explained, "When the brain experiences pain over and over, those neurons get 'wired together,' and they get better and better at firing together. Unfortunately, that means the brain gets better and better at feeling pain."[41] He calls this "neuroplastic pain": when the brain changes in such a way that reinforces chronic pain.

It begins innocently enough. After an acute injury, such as a back sprain, the memory center of the brain begins to create nerve pathways. Once formed, these pathways can remember the back pain even after the muscle sprain has fully healed, and the pain can then become chronic. A life in chronic pain is more than a physical discomfort; it adversely impacts our ability to function in the world as well as our mental health and spiritual well-being. Those who endure debilitating chronic pain tend to suffer in many other ways, as they may be unable to work, fully take care of themselves, or enjoy even simple social and recreational activities.

The medical profession has had limited success treating most chronic pain. Most treatments—including medication, injections, exercise, and relaxation techniques—temporarily relieve the pain but don't eliminate it. A lack of adequate treatment has inadvertently led to the opioid crisis, a more than two-decades-long struggle that has taken or interrupted the lives of millions of people.*

Although the medical community continues to prescribe opioids for pain management, they have become far more cautious and knowledgeable, with many doctors recommending non-opioid approaches such as mindfulness techniques and embodied movement such as qi gong and yoga.

---

* Three factors are sometimes credited with inadvertently setting the stage for the opioid crisis: (1) the American Pain Society's call for hospitals and clinics to add pain assessment as the "fifth vital sign," along with body temperature, pulse, blood pressure, and respiration; (2) research that stated that people prescribed opioids for chronic pain did not get addicted; and (3) the intense marketing of opioid painkillers by pharmaceutical companies.

When we learned through our study that A.W.E. eased chronic pain, we were excited about the potential for A.W.E. as a safe and viable pain intervention. Chronic pain is intimately linked to the autonomic nervous system (ANS), and as we'll explain throughout this book, the A.W.E. Method affects the ANS. For the chronic pain segment of our studies, we asked participants to rate their pain on a scale of 0 to 10 for each of the following:

Back pain
Neck pain
Pain in the extremities (arms, legs, and joints)
Headaches
Chest pain or shortness of breath

Over the three-week study, participants reported a statistically significant decrease in physical pain. There was a direct dose-response relationship, meaning that on days when people reported experiencing more awe, they reported decreased levels of physical pain. Looking at the big trends in the two studies, we observed that awe increased over time and pain decreased over time. The results held true for all types of pain.

These findings have been reinforced by the results Michael has seen with his patients. As a pain management specialist, Michael sees an average of about a thousand patients per year. In the first year that Michael introduced a twenty-one-day A.W.E. program at his clinic, fifty patients went through the program, many of whom experienced life-changing results that have improved their ability to regulate their chronic pain without medication.

Although there is not yet specific research on the mechanisms of how awe improves chronic pain, Michael believes that patients who regularly practice the A.W.E. Method ruminate less about their pain and shift their perspective and reactivity to pain by being less fearful, which helps them relax. The more his patients used the A.W.E. Method, the more their autonomic nervous systems relaxed, decreasing both the perception of pain and the associated muscle spasms. Among Michael's patients, the A.W.E. Method was also beneficial for other types of pain, including neuropathy, autoimmune conditions such as Crohn's disease, and fibromyalgia.[42]

One of Michael's long-term patients, Rebecca, suffered from chronic low back pain after a work injury that resulted in a lumbar spinal fusion. The surgery helped relieve the pain radiating down her legs but caused scar tissue in her lower back. Before she participated in Michael's Power of Awe class, Rebecca was taking morphine three times a day for chronic pain that would otherwise keep her from volunteering at the animal rescue center and enjoying outdoor activities with her husband. By the third group session, she said she was able to begin lowering her morphine for the first time since her back surgery. Three months later, Rebecca told Michael that the A.W.E. Method had given her near total control over her pain and she was able to stop her pain medication. Most importantly, she said, "Now that I'm feeling better, I get to have a double dose of awe from both volunteering with the animals and appreciating quality time with my husband on our daily morning walks."[43]

· · ·

A.W.E. is a quick and easy intervention that can cultivate awe in the ordinary, at any time and in any place. Our findings suggest that cultivating awe for less than a minute a day reduces symptoms of depression and anxiety, improves social connection, decreases loneliness, reduces burnout, lowers stress, increases well-being, and reduces chronic pain. Imagine what more sustained and frequent experiences of awe could do.

We explore the many other benefits of awe in upcoming chapters. But first we want to answer the questions: How can one emotion have such sweeping effects? How are all these changes even possible? Awe, it turns out, is akin to a spoonful of medicine. If we could bottle it, we could help alleviate all manner of suffering. Let's take a closer look.

CHAPTER 2

THE SCIENCE OF HEALING

Every other Wednesday, about forty-five neuroscientists, pain special- ists, psychologists, family doctors, allied health professionals, surgeons, basic science researchers, and educated patients in pain from around the world log on to their computers to meet via Zoom for exactly one hour. The hosts of this meeting, called the Dynamic Healing Discussion Group, are David Hanscom, MD, a retired orthopedic complex spinal deformity surgeon based on the West Coast, and Dr. Stephen Porges, PhD, a distin- guished scientist at Indiana University and professor of psychiatry who has spent years researching psychophysiology—the interaction between mind and body. During the early months of COVID-19, the out-of-the- box thinking of these two doctors led to the formation of this scientific discussion group.

Luminaries in their respective fields, these two men are considered out- liers in the field of medicine because they are committed to bringing the deeply documented—yet mostly overlooked—data regarding the nature of chronic disease into the public domain. By sharing their research, thoughts, and latest findings, this entire group has advanced the science of healing be- yond what any one person would be capable of in such a short time.

Much of their approach is based on the idea that to heal from pain and illness we must feel safe. What does safety have to do with healing? How safe or threatened we feel directly impacts our nervous system and physiological state. Members of this group would argue that, when in a chronic threat-induced response of fight-flight (an activated sympathetic nervous system), the body is consuming its reserves to survive and so lacks the resources for full healing to occur. Full healing happens in the physiological state of feeling safe (when the parasympathetic nervous system, or PNS, is active), which produces a profound shift in the body's chemistry. When the PNS is active, the body is in a "rest and digest" state, or what we like to refer to as "rest and repair" state. Fuel supplies are replenished, tissues are rebuilt, and the body is restored.

Awe, as you'll soon learn, helps us feel safe and therefore contributes to healing.

We joined the group early on. As a pain specialist, Michael was familiar with Dr. Hanscom's work. Jake was eager to learn more about Dr. Porges's theories regarding the nervous system. This group has not only deepened our understanding of the healing process but has also shown us how awe fits into this revolutionary discussion of healing—and why we are getting the results we're getting with A.W.E.

It all starts and ends with whether we feel safe—or under threat.

CYTOKINES: THE BODY'S MASTER COMMUNICATORS

Throughout the body exists a four-billion-year-old communication network that works tirelessly to keep us healthy. "Cytokines" are the master communicators of this intercellular signaling network. Released by the immune system, these small proteins report news to cells located anywhere in the body. Like gossiping neighbors, cytokines ensure that if something is awry, everyone on the block knows. When all is well, cytokines share the good news too.

If the body is under threat by a virus or bacteria, for instance, immune cells release "threat cytokines." They are the buglers, signaling that a battle is about to begin and informing other cells (such as white blood cells) to call in the troops—to increase in numbers and deploy to the site of the invader. Threat cytokines don't really attack invaders but tell other well-equipped immune cells to attack. Once released, threat cytokines trigger a cascade of physiological events, one of which is to create inflammation at the scene of the invasion or injury as a form of protection.

Most everybody has experienced the results of threat cytokines in action. If you've ever suffered from a fever, threat cytokines were involved in activating your immune cells and raising your body temperature to help fight an infection. Likewise, if you've ever sprained an ankle, you may have seen the area around the joint swell. The injured joint tissue releases threat cytokines, causing blood to rush to the injured area, bringing with it white blood cells and other repair mechanisms.

The immune system does not work alone. The body can sense threats to its health and well-being through multiple inputs, including the brain and the entire nervous system. The body is equipped to protect against not only viruses, bacteria, and physical wounds but also *emotional injury*. Feeling shamed by a parent, for instance, will first register in the brain's cortex and then the amygdala, the hypothalamus, and the sympathetic (fight-flight) nervous system before the immune system releases threat cytokines.

Regardless of the source of a threat, threat cytokines turn up the sympathetic nervous system and simultaneously turn down the parasympathetic (rest and repair) nervous system. The body is now on guard and fully prepared to respond to whatever it perceives as a threat.

When the body senses that the acute threat is over and the immune system has done its job, cytokines communicate that it's time to release "safety cytokines." Safety cytokines direct the immune cells to clear out the inflammation, deactivate the sympathetic nervous system, recharge the PNS, and let the healing begin.

Although we are pretty much limiting our discussion of cytokines to communication and inflammation, cytokines are more than markers of an immune response, and the cytokine communication network goes beyond the immune system and inflammation. Cytokines are so important to our well-being that every cell in the body has cytokine receptor sites, giving cytokines widespread—systemic—influence. They affect not only inflammation levels but also metabolism and hormones, for instance.

Although threat cytokines are helpful in stimulating an immune response when necessary, they are also catabolic—they can be highly degenerative. While threat cytokines are busy signaling and creating inflammation, they can also signal for our tissues—organs, muscles, and the like—to be catabolized and used as fuel for the fight-flight response.

Catabolism and degeneration begin when threat cytokines linger for too long at high levels. The cumulative result is that acute inflammation becomes chronic inflammation, and the organism under attack deconstructs and deteriorates.

INFLAMMATION: ACUTE GOOD, CHRONIC BAD

Threat cytokines linger with the intention of helping the body if it, for instance, is regularly exposed to toxins or fails to clear an infection. Sensing an ongoing threat, threat cytokines bind with other chemicals in the body to keep the immune system in operation at a low level. At this point, threat cytokine signaling may become chronic and begin to damage the original site of distress and even healthy parts of the body—organs, tissues, blood vessels. Over time, sometimes months or decades, this low-level rogue response can do a lot of damage and spread to other parts of the body. Making matters worse is that safety cytokines will not turn on until the intercellular communication network indicates that the now chronically out-of-control threat is over.

Chronic inflammation is associated with the root of all chronic diseases, including the three main killers: diabetes, heart disease, and cancer. Chronic threat signaling is marked by not only inflammation and degeneration but also symptoms of fatigue, insomnia, depression, anxiety, loss of libido, gastrointestinal discomfort, joint pain, and more. Its effects can graduate and cause metabolic and autoimmune disorders such as diabetes, lupus, rheumatoid arthritis, and inflammatory bowel disease. And it can be relentless. Cytokine storms, or a sudden and massive release of cytokines into the bloodstream, are most associated with neurodegeneration (think Alzheimer's and Parkinson's) and heart disease. This is threat cytokine catabolism at its worst.

Although everyone experiences temporary inflammation at one time or another, chronic inflammation is a problem in at least 60 percent of people in the United States, and it's a leading cause of death worldwide.[1]

TRAUMA, ANXIETY, AND STRESS: SYNONYMS FOR THREAT

Threat comes in many forms, and the body interprets emotional injury as a threat. Living under consistent threat can inform the sympathetic nervous system to stay active and keep threat cytokines circulating. Because there's no sprained ankle or flu to address, inflammation may be relatively low, but the threat cytokines still keep busy catabolizing.

There are many reasons why we would feel threatened. It's well known that many of us are walking around under a persistent threat response, with a sympathetic nervous system that won't stop. We're tense, stressed, "wired tight" for any number of reasons. Twenty-first-century-style stress (traffic, bank overdraft notices, divorce, pressure to succeed) is often chronic. The result can be unnecessary low-level inflammation wreaking havoc in our body, even if we aren't aware of it.

According to D. R. Clawson, MD (another member of Hanscom's group), Porges, and others, chronic inflammation has social, psychological, and biological causes—many of them rooted in stress—and they argue that we ought to be looking at threat cytokines closely. A high threat cytokine load not only leads to chronic disease but also changes how we act and how we navigate through this world. In an as-yet unpublished paper, they write that threat cytokines, which they refer to as TCs, "are the underpinnings of the majority of chronic physical illnesses and diseases [and] of all mental illnesses and diseases, including addictions." They also note that threat cytokines are elevated in people who have been subject to isolation, crowding, poverty, disenfranchisement, discrimination, and injustice and that "the TC trigger is sensitized and the TC load is frequently elevated in those who have suffered significant past traumas." Ultimately, they conclude that TCs "are responsible for sickness behavior, helplessness and hopelessness."[2]

It's not a stretch to see how trauma and stress can lead to chronic inflammation and disease. Emotional injury activates an immune response, and more than the flu or a broken bone, emotional injury tends to stay with us. Most people have a resentment or two they hold onto, or they haven't fully recovered from being judged by someone whose opinion they care about. Any degree of emotional pain can set off physiological events.

In a University of California, Irvine, study that looked at whether feeling judged by others could increase proinflammatory cytokine activity, researchers asked a group of healthy females to complete a speech and math task before an audience that would evaluate their performance. A control group performed the same tasks without an audience. The evaluated group showed increased levels of a proinflammatory cytokine and reduced response levels of glucocorticoids, which help quell an inflammatory response. The control group showed no changes in proinflammatory activity.[3]

According to Hanscom's group, full recovery from anything, including depression, anxiety, stress, burnout, and chronic pain—all conditions we measured for in our studies—cannot be achieved as long as threat cytokine levels remain high because the body doesn't have the necessary resources for healing. "Anything" also includes every mental and physical disease state in the book, from Alzheimer's to the zoster virus (shingles). When we talked to Clawson in a Zoom interview, he shared how he sees threat cytokines as contributing to all types of health conditions, including, for example, the obesity epidemic:

We have a false model of obesity and diabetes. Our model has been for years, too many calories in and not enough calories out. And then we kind of have recently said, well, it might be the quality of the calories we're putting in. But when you track it a little deeper, you realize that people who live in chronic threat have impaired fat metabolism and insulin resistance. In advanced threat, they actually conserve more energy. They're going to accumulate fat eating very little, and I've seen that in the hospital over my entire career. I didn't know what it was. They would be eating like birds. And they were actually eating relatively decent diets, but they were still morbidly obese. And unfortunately, we criticize those people by saying, "Well, you know, they can't push themselves away from the table." But it's really a threat-related disease. And then diabetes. The threat cytokines cause insulin resistance and hyperglycemia. And what's also so interesting is these cytokines. Their goal is to mobilize as much sugar for the battle as possible.

To take it to another level, we need to move obese people into a sense of safety that may be beyond basic medical care. We have to essentially change culture to become healthy again.[4]

AWE AND SAFETY CYTOKINES: THE PARASYMPATHETIC SYSTEM STEPS UP

Whether caused by strep throat, coronavirus, a sprained ankle, stress, or shame, inflammation can become chronic if the sympathetic nervous system continues to dominate. To lower inflammation, increase immunity, improve metabolism, and prevent further damage to tissues and organs—to heal whatever ails us—we must control the proinflammatory threat cytokine response and increase production of the anti-inflammatory *safety* cytokines, which support health and wellness. When safety cytokines are elevated, the parasympathetic response (the body's rest and repair state) activates. According to Clawson's paper:

> It is here where we are anti-inflammatory, anabolic, regenerative, restorative, connected, bonded, sexual, reproductive, intellectual, and creative. We also have strong cellular immunity. Our immune cells change phenotypes [their physical expression] when in safety and become active not only in immunity but are fundamental to the regeneration and recovery process. We must get to this state to fully heal. We are energized and we feel well when fully safe, seen and secure.[5]

Completing the healing cycle requires more than just interrupting the cause of acute inflammation (taking antibiotics to kill streptococcal bacteria, for instance). Safety cytokines must be activated.

Awe, it turns out, is the *only* positive emotion known to *significantly* decrease proinflammatory (threat) cytokines and increase anti-inflammatory (safety) cytokines, as measured by interleukin 6 (IL-6) levels.

IL-6 is one of many types of cytokine and functions primarily as a proinflammatory (threat) cytokine. In communication with other cells and chemicals in the body, IL-6 stimulates inflammatory pathways to protect against infection and injury. IL-6 also poses a special risk: it can facilitate turning acute inflammation into chronic inflammation.

In a study that measured IL-6 levels in college students before they were asked to fill out the Positive and Negative Affect Schedule, a tool that measures how often a person feels positive or negative emotions, those students who were generally more positive had lower levels of IL-6. When these same researchers performed a second study using the Dispositional Positive Emotions Scale and the Big Five Personality Inventory, they found that awe predicted lower levels of IL-6, even over other big positive emotions such as gratitude, generosity, joy, and love.[6]

Without referring to cytokines, in *The Book of Hope*, famed wildlife scientist and author Jane Goodall tells a story that illustrates how living under threat creates hopelessness and physical pain rooted in inflammation and how awe, by bringing us back to safety, creates healing.

The story centers around Cunsolo, an Inuit woman who was writing her dissertation about how the Inuit—indigenous people of Alaska, Northern Canada, and Greenland—were losing their way of life. After hearing so many stories of sadness and despair from tribal members, Cunsolo felt their emotional pain. One day, she found she could no longer type—she had suddenly developed debilitating nerve pain in her arms and hands. Cunsolo had experienced such grief during the interview process that she became physically ill.

Several specialists could find nothing physically wrong with her. So she visited an Inuit elder, who told her she needed to find *awe* and joy every day as a means to letting go of her grief. Cunsolo made a point to find awe in nature every day, and within weeks her nerve pain was gone.

The stories Cunsolo was documenting had activated her sympathetic nervous system—she empathized with her interviewees to the point where she felt under threat, just as the people she was interviewing were feeling. By experiencing awe every day, she was able to calm her nervous system, turn off the threat cytokines, and produce safety cytokines.

Awe isn't the only means of lowering threat cytokines and increasing safety cytokines. Individually, we can help others feel safe through the smallest of gestures, by greeting them with a smile and a kind voice and posture, for instance. These welcoming expressions signal to others that they are safe with us and can let their guard down. Relaxation techniques such as meditation and feeling welcome in a safe community have the same effect—they promote recovery. But some people find it difficult to meditate, and many others feel isolated and as if they don't belong. Awe, on the other hand, is available to everyone who tries the A.W.E. Method.

How we get sick and whether we heal completely involve a much more complex interaction of cells and systems within the body than we've described here. But researchers are learning that, regardless of the source of chronic inflammation, healing can happen when the body senses safety. Awe gives us that. As our studies showed, the more we access it, the better we feel.

Neal Kearney, one of Michael's patients, shared the following story about how awe takes away his chronic pain:

At the tender age of seven I was introduced to surfing, bright eyes brimming with awe at the power of the waves, the smell of the sea, and the weightless, flying feeling I got when my Godfather pushed me into those first waves. As I grew up in Santa Cruz, I joined a group of young surfers pushing themselves and each other to win contests and attain sponsorship. It turned from an ethereal pursuit to a dog-eat-dog, competitive lifestyle. With all this pressure to perform, the moments of awe began to come fewer and far between.

When I began to suffer from chronic pain I was twenty years old. I became immersed in my suffering, dulling the sharp edges of reality with painkillers, self-imposed isolation, video games, and sleep. I started surfing less and less. My arthritic spine and hips diminished my skills, and I became less physically able to get out and enjoy the love of my life. I was completely numb with pain, grief, and anger. Eventually I stopped surfing and avoided driving by the coastline for a whole year, attempting to cope with my loss.

I'm thirty-five now. Over the past decade I've studied, practiced, and taught mindfulness and yoga extensively. I had both my hips replaced last year, which has enabled me to get back in the water. With my new limitations, the old pressure to perform has dissipated. Rather than choosing to rip the wave to pieces, I've begun to slow myself down and stay present throughout the entire process.

I can no longer do an explosive aerial maneuver, but by God, how beautiful it is to notice the shimmering reflection of the sun as it bounces off the spray! How might it feel if I took a moment from time to time to fully experience the depths of bliss available to me while sliding down the face of a cresting wave fueled by energy produced thousands of miles away? When I use my beginner's mind, I'm able to tap into the immeasurable awe found in abundance in the sea, and for those fleeting moments pain is the furthest thing from my mind.[7]

The capacity to help heal the mind and body is only one of awe's superpowers. In the next chapter, we look at other reasons why the emotion of awe has been getting so much attention.

CHAPTER 3

UNVEILING AWE

In the upper reaches of pleasure and on the boundary of fear is a little studied emotion—awe. . . . Fleeting and rare, experiences of awe can change the course of a life in profound and permanent ways. Yet the field of emotion research is almost silent with respect to awe.

—Dacher Keltner and Jonathan Haidt, "Approaching
Awe, a Moral, Spiritual, and Aesthetic Emotion"

Awe has been garnering a lot of attention as of late. It's the subject of books, workshops, articles in major newspapers and magazines, TED Talks, podcasts, YouTube presentations, and more and more journal articles. Some companies are using the word in their branding. Even developers and architects are considering how to evoke awe when doing everything from designing digital devices to enhancing museum experiences. But it wasn't always this way.

A deep and thorough understanding of awe has been a long time coming, mostly because social psychologists traditionally viewed awe as insignificant to human development. They didn't think it served a purpose. Awe researcher Michelle Shiota from Arizona State University compared the perception of awe to a luxury item: "Awe is often thought of as the Gucci handbag of emotions. It's nice if you can afford one, but that handbag is not something people actually need."[1] Or so they used to think.

A host of researchers, including Shiota, have been confirming that awe is more of a necessity than an indulgence. An abundance of studies on awe have cropped up in recent years, and the findings suggest that the implications of the emotion are enormous. According to leading awe researcher Dacher Keltner, "There are a lot of reasons to be bullish [about awe.]"[2]

Awe, we now know, can help us discover new meaning—figure out what we might enjoy doing in our lives, improve levels of satisfaction, and reinterpret (or better understand) painful experiences.[3] For instance, Kirk Schneider, a humanistic psychologist and author of several books on awe, uses awe in his psychotherapy practice to help clients move through difficult feelings. "I try to support people to stay present to their pain, to their difficulty, to the point where they can come into larger parts of themselves and are no longer as threatened by that pain. I talk about it as the gradual shift from abject terror and paralysis to incremental intrigue and curiosity . . . to actual wonder and even fascination by what their experience has opened them to."[4]

The health benefits of awe that we covered in Chapters 1 and 2, from reducing depression and anxiety to promoting well-being, are driving physicians such as Michael to prescribe awe to their patients. And in his therapy practice, Jake is using awe as an effective intervention to alter patients' self-esteem and improve their relationships.

Awe is worth exploring—not just for the fleeting sense of elation it offers but because of the lasting benefits. There are many explanations for why we need awe in our emotional toolkit. In addition to the benefits we covered earlier, researchers have learned that awe does the following:

- Encourages curiosity
- Inspires energy, especially when experienced in nature
- Quiets the mind's "monkey chatter"
- Calms the nervous system

- Reduces inflammation
- Makes us less materialistic and more generous
- Increases spirituality as we experience being part of something larger than the self
- Diminishes our sense of self so that we are less self-absorbed
- Softens hard-core convictions, making us more open-minded and less rigid in our thinking
- Leaves us feeling more present and patient
- Leads us to be more friendly, humble, and connected to others
- Improves life satisfaction

All these benefits are worthwhile in and of themselves. When combined, they make us better, more interesting people, which helps us achieve what most of us long for yet are perpetually baffled by: awe helps us improve our relationships and inspires us to feel happy, even thrilled, with being alive.

So why did it take researchers so long to bring awe into the laboratory?

UNVEILING AWE

The science of awe is young, going on just a quarter of a century. Although there has been a long-standing interest in human potential and positive psychology, when it comes to emotions, psychologists have tended to look more closely at the so-called negative aspects of human behavior. For decades, there was a fight-flight bias among researchers, who believed that we benefited most by understanding emotions that deeply affect our survival instincts—negative emotions such as fear and anger, for instance.

That bias shifted in the late 1990s when the scientific community found value in understanding the role positive emotions have played in our evolution. And, as you'll soon discover, the role they play is substantive.

It took another few years before anyone started looking closely at the grandest of positive emotions—awe. They weren't saving the best for last. Rather, they struggled with some fundamental questions—namely, how do you describe something as complex as awe?

For example, unlike the very one-dimensional emotions of happiness and fear, awe can be both a positive and a negative emotion. Whether we feel euphoria or dread depends entirely on the context in which the emotion arises—whether we're in wonder of something we value, appreciate, or find amazing, or we feel a sense of terror or veneration over being in the presence of that which appears so dauntingly powerful it frightens us.

THE TWO FACES OF AWE

Awe is really two different emotions that have historically shared the same name. But they are not the same. Threat-based awe and positive-based awe originate in different parts of the brain.

In a study that used awe-inspiring videos and neuroimaging (functional MRI) to show which areas of the brain lit up during experiences of threat-based awe versus positive-based awe, researchers found relevant distinctions. When feeling under threat, the left middle temporal gyrus (MTG) connected strongly with the amygdala, which processes threatening experiences. When feeling positive, the MTG connected strongly with the anterior and posterior cingulate cortex, both of which are involved with the reward process, and the supramarginal gyrus, which is involved with the expression of admiration and compassion.[5]

The only similarities between threat-based and positive-based awe are the degree to which they may impact us—and how hard they can be to describe. Both are very powerful, but we're going to focus primarily on the one that we all want more of.

How we use the word *awe* has changed over the centuries. Ancient history paints a dark picture of the emotion. The first use of the word may have been in Old Norse. At the time, and for centuries, awe was used to describe the terror associated with being in the presence of a divine being. Awe was also considered a source of what some people might think of as "the fear of God"—a reverence for that which could deliver a divine punishment if we didn't behave or act accordingly. The Bible uses the Hebrew word *yirah*, which translates to the kind of awe that evokes either fear or joy and wonder, encouraging us to be "stunned and amazed" by God (Isaiah 29:9) or in wonder of God's miracles. Or to "Let all the earth fear the Lord; Let all the inhabitants of the world stand in awe of Him" (Psalms 33:8).

By the Age of Enlightenment, the definition of awe had softened, at least in the English language.* In the 1700s, awe was used to describe experiences associated with not necessarily religion but the extraordinary within the familiar or the beautiful: the sound of thunder or the music produced by a symphony orchestra. This definition was based on the idea that these experiences were miraculous. Today, the meaning of awe has pretty much done an about-face from its ancient origins. Though awe can still describe terror, it's more commonly used when referring to astonishingly positive, breathtaking experiences.

Beyond defining awe, researchers struggled with how to bring awe into the lab. If awe is associated with being in the presence of someone or something extraordinary, would researchers have to bring the lab and study participants to one of the Seven Wonders of the World? In addition, awe also tends to be a fleeting emotion and therefore hard to capture. How would you measure it? Researchers eventually got around these challenges (as we learned in Chapter 1). But initially, for these reasons, awe was sidestepped as a subject of study. But not forgotten.

---

* In Dutch, the words for awe, *ontzag* and *vrees*, still denote fear, reverence, or terror, which make it challenging for researchers in the Netherlands to study the positive effects of awe.

A FRESH LOOK AT AWE

While sitting on a deck overlooking San Francisco one day in the late 1980s, Dacher Keltner, a young graduate student at the University of California, San Francisco, and his psychology professor, Paul Ekman, were talking when Keltner asked what he should study. Ekman, whose eyes cast over the San Francisco cityscape, with the bay and ocean as a backdrop, said, "Awe." Ekman planted a seed.[6]

More than a decade later, Keltner, now working at the University of California, Berkeley, and social psychologist Jonathan Haidt, a professor at New York University, came out with a 2003 landmark paper describing awe as a "moral, spiritual, and aesthetic emotion." Not only did they define awe by researching the word's origins, but they also established a framework for how to study this most magnificent of emotions.

Keltner and Haidt did something else to help set the stage for the explosion of awe research that soon followed. They distinguished awe from other emotions by distilling the experience down to two essential mechanisms. To experience awe, they said, requires vastness, or the feeling that we are part of something much larger than ourselves, and cognitive accommodation, or the sudden ability to change our perspective. Later, researchers determined two additional features of awe: Awe expands our perception of time and increases our propensity to be prosocial—to connect with other people, participate in community, and even do what's best for the group rather than the individual. These four mechanisms of awe are responsible not only for many of the benefits of awe but also for our continued existence as a species. Without these features of awe, our evolution may have been cut short, as you'll soon learn.

Do we need to experience all four of these mechanisms to be in awe? We like to think of these features like musical notes. If you hit one of them, it's a note. When you hit three of them, it's a chord. If you hit four of them, it's another chord. Each note or chord has a different sound and feel—a different flavor. Awe, then, is experienced in different ways to different degrees by different people. We'll dive thoroughly into the spectrum of awe experiences in Chapter 11. For now, we hope you're curious enough to explore vastness, cognitive accommodation, time perception, and prosocial behaviors so that you can recognize them when you experience awe.

VASTNESS: AN EXPANSIVE EXPERIENCE

Typically, *vastness* is used to describe something large or boundless. We might think of a vast landscape. But when talking about the vastness of awe, we're not referring to the *source* of awe but rather *the state of being* in which awe puts us. In the context of awe, vastness is anything that gives us the sense that we are in the presence of something larger than the self—an *experience outside our normal range of experiences.*

Although a vast, spectacular view can deliver awe, it's not a requirement for feeling the emotional note of vastness. The vastness of awe is a vastness within yourself.

The breakthrough in our research, as demonstrated with the A.W.E. Method, is that the vastness of awe can be found in the ordinary. The simple act of giving attention to the veins in a maple tree leaf or watching a toddler play with childlike wonder can set us on a track to experiencing awe, giving us a sense that we are part of something much bigger and expanding our awareness of what it means to be a part of this world.

There is value in experiencing vastness, as it has the potential to be personally and powerfully life changing. Feeling that we are part of something bigger than our self means we feel smaller. Our ego diminishes a bit—in a good way—making room for other perspectives.

When our sense of self decreases, you might think we would feel that what we're doing is less important or less significant. But there's a paradox: as our sense of self diminishes, we feel more significant in other ways. It's counterintuitive, but when we connect to something larger—whether it's nature, our place of work, a political movement, or God or a universal energy—our orientation in the world shifts. We feel momentum, and we sense we are moving with the momentum. We aren't just on our own anymore. Something is happening, and we are part of it. We feel connected.

On a personal level, as we become less self-absorbed, less narcissistic, and take ourselves less seriously, we relax. The pressure to stand out or be special or compete dissipates and is replaced by humility. There's something very comforting about being humble. It's a soothing emotion. Our focus is more outward, and we communicate more easily and naturally with other people. Conversations are more pleasant, productive, and meaningful.

Michael tells a story of receiving large doses of humility from some of our planet's smallest creatures. During a period when he felt burned out in his career, he and a group of his whitewater-rafting friends ventured down the Colorado River into the depths of the Grand Canyon. In addition to having an epic nineteen-day adventure, one of their objectives was to participate in citizen science, collecting bugs for climate change research.

Every evening, the group shone a bright light to attract the bugs into their collection kit. In these moments, an entire cosmos of insects came to life. The number and variety of bugs were astonishing—all different shapes, colors, and sizes of insects appeared, seemingly out of nowhere, all headed toward a shared universal calling card: light.

Michael expected the canyon's 1.8-billion-year-old layers of geological formations to bring him awe. Never once did he imagine that swarms of tiny insects would leave him feeling connected to something bigger than himself. There Michael was, surrounded by thousands of living beings he'd had no awareness of until he turned on the light. Throughout his trip, he had been oblivious to their existence because he was lost in his thoughts. When the bugs came to life, so did Michael. His sense of self diminished while his perspective expanded. He and his troubles were not as big as he'd been making them out to be. And his life was more meaningful and satisfying than he'd been imagining.

Michael worked (and played) hard on this trip, and he went home feeling refreshed. Although the vastness he experienced as part of awe was temporary, Michael carried his more enlightened perspective—and the memory of the awe-inspiring insects—into his everyday life.

THINK ABOUT IT . . .

Have you ever felt yourself to be a small part of a big movement or project with a group of people who could accomplish more than you could accomplish on your own?

Have you ever felt the momentum of being part of a movement or special practice where you didn't personally stand out, but the experience was personally significant?

Have you ever been lost, or felt small, in the grandeur of nature? Think of what it would feel like to climb to the top of a pine tree that's swaying in the wind in the forest.

Have you ever been present when a baby is born or when someone or something dies?

Vastness does something more than make us feel connected. It is an expansion, creating the space we need to see things differently. While in vastness, we may feel a subtle disruption to our perceptions, what's known as cognitive accommodation. It's as if a light bulb switches on, inspiring new ways of thinking.

COGNITIVE ACCOMMODATION:
CREATING NEW PERCEPTIONS

Cognitive accommodation is perhaps the most intriguing feature of awe. Awe-filled experiences can disrupt our conceptions, or how we perceive, view, understand, and make meaning of ourselves and the world around us. To make sense of an awe-filled experience, which feels new and inspiring, our understanding shifts or expands so that we perceive and comprehend more than our little silo of the world. The shift is cognitive—it involves how we think. It's also subtle and quick—a slight but noticeable disorientation that causes us to stop and wonder. Or to rethink what we "know" to be true.

To accommodate this shift—to make sense of it—we see a bigger, enhanced picture. And this can change how we approach something, such as nature. The world today might be a different place, for example, if John Muir, naturalist, conservationist, and founder of the Sierra Club, hadn't experienced cognitive accommodation—what we like to call an "awe-piphany"—one day in college at the University of Wisconsin, Madison.

While sitting outside, a classmate from Muir's botany class presented Muir with a flower from a black locust tree and explained that the tree is a member of the pea family. Muir was astounded. How was it that the black locust, which can reach heights of a hundred feet, could be a member of the legume family when the pea plant measures, at most, eight feet tall? When Muir wrote his autobiography fifty years later, he recalled that moment:

> This fine lesson charmed me and sent me flying to the woods and meadows in wild enthusiasm. Like everybody else I was always fond of flowers, attracted by their external beauty and purity. Now my eyes were opened to their inner beauty, all alike revealing glorious traces of the thoughts of God, and leading on and on into the infinite cosmos.[7]

John Muir went on to help establish several national parks, including Yosemite and the Grand Canyon.

Some awe studies have looked at how cognitive accommodation affects our attachment to ideas or convictions. Specifically, researchers have considered individuals' willingness to let go of hard-core beliefs around topics such as religion and social justice—subjects about which people tend to be absolute. Many people won't budge when it comes to how they feel about God or a political party or climate change, for instance. In awe, because we experience cognitive accommodation, we are more willing to look at our convictions with an open mind and even humility.[8]

We question our beliefs—not out of force or obligation but from a place of genuine curiosity or "not knowing"—which leads to new understandings and often a reevaluation. Loosening our attachment to our beliefs and ideals helps us revisit them with a fresh perspective. This doesn't necessarily mean we give up on our ideals or back down when standing up for what we know is right. It means that we approach our beliefs with an open heart and mind. In this way, we allow other perspectives to enter our psyche, which ultimately results in a more holistic perspective.

Awe can also make us feel less attached to ideas, perceptions, and even possessions. Several studies have concluded that awe helps us rise above the need to accumulate wealth and material possessions.[9]

The cognitive accommodation in awe also improves our relationships and interactions with others. People find us easier to be around, and because we are less judgmental, we are more likely to enjoy being in the company of others. When both parties to an interaction have the capacity to accommodate, the result is refreshing. Jake offers an honest look at how cognitive accommodation helped him overcome a bias he didn't know he had.

Years ago, when Layla first walked into Jake's office, he was taken a little off guard. Layla was not typical of his clients—dressed in a biker outfit and covered in tattoos, Layla appeared angry and defensive. She had spent the last twenty years in prison for murder, and now that she'd been released, her main reason for attending therapy was to figure out what to do for a living. Layla was also in recovery from drug and alcohol addiction. Jake was a bit daunted by the unfamiliarity of Layla's circumstances but up for the challenge.

Helping Layla turned out to be far easier and more rewarding than Jake had initially imagined it might be. And he quickly grew to appreciate Layla for who she was—not who he thought she was. During his sessions with Layla, Jake was in awe that someone could be so different from his first impressions.

Layla was an example of what the human spirit is capable of. At this point in her life, she was gifted at witnessing other people without judging them. She had created a wide-open space—lots of room for cognitive accommodation—to see people and the world in new ways, even in the most extreme situations.

Jake experienced cognitive accommodation just by being in her presence, and he imagined that she could elicit this in others. Given her aptitude for seeing people and events freshly, Jake suggested she explore becoming an addictions counselor. If a client ever claimed they had sunk too low to recover, Layla's personal story was testimony to the contrary. And because of her life experiences, she stimulated others to open their minds and rethink what was possible. Layla could be a beacon of hope to those who felt hopeless.

Layla didn't come across as someone who was impressed with herself. But she was impressive. She became a caring, compassionate counselor. Layla has spent the last decade or so giving people the space and permission they need to heal.

THINK ABOUT IT . . .

Have you ever had a belief or preconceived notion about something and then completely changed your mind as you learned more about it?

Have you ever judged someone who turned out to come to your aid or be very different from what you thought?

Have you ever had a phobia that boxed you in and then overcame that phobia?

Have you ever insisted that you were right only to find out that you weren't?

Cognitive accommodation is remarkable in that it can change how we think and feel about any number of things, including what many of us feel we have too little of: time. In the awe experience, perhaps somewhere between vastness and cognitive accommodation, we experience time differently. In awe, our perception of time expands.

PERCEPTION OF TIME

Most of us have experienced the sensation of some moments flying by while others seem to drag on. On some days, we almost feel forced to kill time. Maybe we've a few hours before an event we're nervous about or not looking forward to. We're dressed well ahead of schedule, then twiddling our thumbs as we anxiously wait for our ride. While deeply absorbed in a project, on the other hand, we might forget about time altogether. We're in the flow or in the zone, feeling one with whatever it is we're doing, energized and enjoying the process. When we finally do look at the clock, hours may have passed, much to our surprise. This is a terrific, productive state to be in. But where *did* the time go?

Researchers have long equated how we interpret the passing of time with how we're feeling at the time. When our activities are pleasurable and we're happy, time seems to go fast. If we're depressed, anxious, or lonely, time seems to slow to a crawl. When in awe, however, we don't experience time at all: our sense of time is suspended.

Other positive emotional states don't deliver this same altered perception of time. In what is to date the most relevant study of time perception and awe, researchers showed participants awe-inspiring videos of massive waterfalls or people interacting with huge animals. The researchers found that awe moments are not only enjoyable but also enjoyable for what seem like longer moments. Being in these awe moments gave participants the perception that time was abundant. It passed more slowly. The study attributed this sense of abundance to being in the moment—participants who felt awe described being fully present.[10] It's as if awe were designed to be savored.

Awe creates a sense of timelessness, a space that feels eternal, as if there were no beginning or end. In our busy society where most people feel overwhelmed and view time as a scarce commodity, timelessness is a welcome respite. By elongating the moments, awe takes that feeling of overwhelm away. Having experienced awe, we get more done in less time without feeling rushed. And how we connect with others improves dramatically. Feeling and acting as if time were abundant rather than scarce changes the tone of our relationships.

Awe takes away the sense of urgency many of us carry through a busy day by keeping us in the present moment, which calms the sympathetic nervous system. In this space, with urgency out of the picture, we can experience patience. If I'm in relationship with you, and I am more patient with you and connect with you, imagine how that's going to change the tone of our conversations, which in turn is going to shift our attitudes and perspectives. Now we're relating from a fundamentally different place, a place opposite that of urgency and lack—a place of abundance.

THINK ABOUT IT . . .

Do you recall a time when you felt time had expanded?
Have you ever lost track of time?
Have you ever experienced time standing still?
Can you remember when you were a child and you were told you
    had to wait to open a gift?

Beyond these three features of awe—vastness, cognitive accommodation, and the perception of time expanding—researchers have also looked at awe with an eye to whether it has played a role in our social evolution. Why, they wondered, do we feel awe? They found that the evolutionary implications of awe are rewarding as well as central to our survival. These researchers learned that perhaps the greatest benefit of awe to the human race is its propensity to make us behave in ways that encourage getting along with others.

OUR EVOLUTIONARY SUPERPOWER: CONNECTION

Dutch historian and author Rutger Bregman has written about people's potential for goodness. To uncover this potential, he looked back to the ancients. In his book entitled *Humankind: A Hopeful History*, one of the basic questions he asks is, What traits have given *Homo sapiens* an evolutionary advantage? Although Bregman doesn't speak to awe directly, he links human survival to our capacity to connect with others. Bregman writes: "Humans, in short, are anything but poker-faced. We constantly leak emotions and are hardwired to relate to the people around us. But far from being a handicap, this is our true superpower."[11]

Evolution favored prosocial behaviors, giving credence to the theory that emotions that induce the desire to get along with others were, and still are, important to our survival. For our ancestors, living in a tribe offered more protection from enemies and some of the harsh realities of nature. And the group efforts required of hunting and gathering—and later planting and harvesting crops—helped ensure everyone in the group had full bellies. But to live in such proximity to others, we had to be friendly, lest we be kicked out of the tribe and left to fend for ourselves—bleak odds at best.

The more we are able to live in community—to play well with others, so to speak—the better our chances of survival. Awe accomplishes this by encouraging kindness, generosity, and caring behaviors. Awe makes us better people.

In a "survival of the friendliest" theory, Soviet scientist Dmitry Belyaev proclaimed that being a nice person might have contributed to whether we had a mate with whom to procreate—the ultimate assurance that our species would survive. As director of the Institute of Cytology and Genetics in Novosibirsk, the capital of Siberia, beginning in the 1950s Belyaev spent decades breeding captive silver foxes. His goal was to understand the role genetics played in domesticating animals. Over the years, working near the either frozen or mosquito-laden swamps of the Siberian plains, Belyaev and his team bred hundreds of silver foxes, mixing and matching partners by personality traits. When a friendly fox was bred with another friendly fox, the result was an even friendlier fox.

After several generations, the most affable foxes had been domesticated to the point of resembling dogs—wagging their tails and otherwise showing affection toward humans. These foxes had been tamed, not by a trainer but by breeding alone. Belyaev likely demonstrated how our ancient ancestors turned the wild wolf into "man's best friend."

Aside from understanding how domestication takes place, Belyaev came up with his survival of the friendliest theory to explain the proliferation of the human race, suggesting that "people are domesticated apes [and that] . . . the nicest humans had the most kids."[12]

We want to suggest that friendliness relates to awe because awe leads us to be more prosocial and altruistic. Likewise, prosocial behaviors lead us toward awe. If we are kind, generous, and patient—in other words, friendly and connected with others—we are more likely to experience awe spontaneously. It's a continuous feedback loop.

The opposite is also true. When we move away from a prosocial state, relating to others becomes more difficult.

THE LOVE DRUG AND AWE

Oxytocin, a hormone released during childbirth, breastfeeding, hugging, and orgasm, can make us feel euphoric, leading some people to call it the "love drug" or "love hormone." It's likely that the body also releases oxytocin when we are in awe.

In a Duke University study, researchers administered the love drug to one group of men. The control group received a placebo. Both groups were then asked to meditate and answer questions about what emotions they were feeling as well as what they thought about spirituality. Those in the oxytocin group were more likely to report feeling a strong connection to others and that spirituality was important. These men also reported feeling awe and other positive emotions during meditation.[13]

Most people long for connection not only with other people but also with the world at large. Bregman writes that "Our distant ancestors . . . from the coldest tundras to the hottest deserts, believed that everything is connected. They saw themselves as a part of something much bigger, linked to all other animals, plants and Mother Earth. . . . Human beings crave togetherness and interaction. Our spirits yearn for connection just as our bodies hunger for food."[14]

The emotion of awe invites us to connect with others, and many studies support this idea. For instance, one study used an intervention known as "awe walks" to test the effect of awe on a group of aging adults. Perhaps no other age group is more affected by social disconnection than older adults, and so awe researchers turned to this cohort to look at the effect awe had on feelings of social connection.

Over a period of eight weeks, sixty participants spent fifteen minutes walking outdoors every week. One group took awe walks, during which time they were instructed to look with childlike wonder for the novel along their route. The control group was asked to simply walk. Not surprisingly, the awe group reported experiencing joy and other positive emotions during their walks, which increased their sense of being socially connected. They even smiled more.[15]

Feeling connected is also good for our physical health. Researchers at the University of North Carolina determined that even *perceiving* that we have positive social connections leads to improved physical health. For this study, researchers used a form of meditation to induce positive emotions (including awe) and measured the effect on heart rate in a lab using spectral frequency analysis.

For six weeks, one group of participants practiced loving-kindness meditation, a contemplative practice that requires self-generating thoughts of love and goodwill toward others. The participants weren't actually being social with other people when meditating but were just thinking about others lovingly. The control group used no intervention.

Meanwhile, the researchers measured cardiac vagal tone in all participants. *Vagal tone* is a term used to describe the activity of the vagus nerve.

Vagus comes from the Latin word for "wandering." It's a descriptor of how the nerve winds from the brain all the way down to the abdomen. As the longest cranial nerve in the body, the vagus has many responsibilities. It affects everything from facial expressions, voice tonality, and hearing to blood pressure, ability to swallow, and how well our bowels work.

Cardiac vagal tone reflects how the vagus nerve is affecting cardiac functioning. It's possible to measure cardiac vagal tone by looking at heart rate variability (HRV). If you wear any type of fitness tracker on your wrist, you may be familiar with HRV, which is an indicator of how well your body is handling stress. A high HRV, or a varied time lapse between heartbeats, is good, indicating that the nervous system is responding well to life's everyday stressors—including situations such as isolation and illness—and that you are generally feeling positive.

A high vagal tone is good, indicating that the vagus nerve is maintaining healthy blood pressure, blood sugar, and anxiety levels, as well as aiding in digestion. Vagal tone is highest when we feel safe—that is, when we are not in the fight-flight response or under stress. When we do experience stress, a high vagal tone helps us relax more quickly. High vagal tone also indicates low inflammation and lower risk of having a heart attack.

If you recall our discussion of cytokines and awe in Chapter 2, you might find it interesting that HRV is a good marker for threat cytokine load. As the threat cytokine load goes up, HRV falls. The opposite is also true: As safety cytokine load goes up, HRV levels rise. In short, these "high" measurements of vagal tone and HRV tell us that our bodies are handling stress well and that we have a reduced mortality risk—we will likely live longer.

In the loving-kindness meditation study, the researchers found that even perceiving ourselves as socially connected leads to feeling positive emotions (higher HRV and vagal tone), which leads to improved health. And they learned that the reverse is also true: Good health leads to feeling more positive emotions. They called this effect a "self-sustaining upward-spiral dynamic."[16]

Much has been learned about connection and longevity. After reviewing 148 studies on the subject, Brigham Young University researchers considered which factors contributed most to longevity among a group of middle-aged adults. Topping the list was not health, diet, or exercise but having casual conversations with people at the grocery store or at the bus stop, for instance. These types of encounters, which are typically not stressful, promoted a sense of belonging and connection. Coming in at number two were close relationships, or relationships with the people we could count on to be there for us when we needed them.[17] Although this study and others like it did not look at awe, they substantiate the idea that connection is central to our existence and well-being. And as we know from our own research, experiencing awe for less than a minute a day is an effective antidote to loneliness.

AN A.W.E. MOMENT

One of the most remarkable aspects of awe is its ability to help us feel more connected to others. And—similar to the loving-kindness meditation used in the University of North Carolina study—one of the most remarkable aspects of A.W.E. is its ability to generate feelings of connection while we are completely alone.

When you can, find a place where you can be alone and then use the A.W.E. Method while thinking of a person who has been most dear to you in your life. They may be living or they may have passed away. Take time to create a clear picture of that person, maybe a particular memory or scene that captures their essence.

Hold the image in your mind, give it your full attention.

Wait the length of a full inhalation, or maybe more than one, while you take time to appreciate this person. Imagine looking into their eyes.

Consider what they mean to you, what you learned from them, or how you grew as a result of knowing them.

(continues)

(continued)

We can be in the moment while remembering. While you re-member and feel, just remember and feel.

Then, when you're ready, exhale fully and allow yourself a mo-ment of awe.

THINK ABOUT IT . . .

Have you experienced awe and as part of that experience felt more connected to other people, nature, a deity, or yourself or your body?

Have you experienced awe and felt more generous?

Have you ever reconnected with someone you care about after many years apart and felt awe at how easy it was to pick up where you left off?

Have you ever connected so deeply with another species that you felt awe?

We explore many of the other benefits of awe in upcoming chapters. But first we want to answer a couple of questions: How can one emotion have such sweeping effects? How are all these changes even possible? We were curious ourselves. We answered these questions by breaking down the A.W.E. Method to see what changes might be going on in the brain and body. What we learned was affirming—and nothing short of awesome.

PART II

HOW A.W.E. WORKS

CHAPTER 4

A–ATTENTION: RENDERING OUR REALITY

A true Renaissance man, Leonardo da Vinci is most remembered for being a brilliant painter, engineer, and scientist. As accomplished as he was, he also left reams of work unfinished and had poor follow-through. But when something he found to be interesting, important, or beautiful caught his attention, he did more than take notice. He would dig deep, unearth the minutiae, and give his full attention to every speck of detail. He often found amazement in the ordinary, especially when it came to anatomy. His hyper-focused attention to the muscles in the lips led to the *Mona Lisa* and the *Salvator Mundi*, works of art still talked about for the subjects' mysterious smiles—or are they frowns?

THE A.W.E. METHOD

Attention means focusing your full and undivided attention on something you appreciate, value, or find amazing. Look

(continues)

(continued)

around the room you're in. Find that special beautiful some-
thing that you value and appreciate. Look at it closely. Really
look. If it's a small object, pick it up and begin to notice ev-
erything about it. If it's a plant, touch the leaves; notice the
texture, color, and smell; and notice the life inside it. If it's a
painting, imagine the painter painting it and notice the depth,
light, and colors.

Wait means slowing down or pausing. So take a breath—
inhale deeply while you appreciate this cherished item in
your home.

The final step, **Exhale and Expand**, amplifies whatever
sensations you are experiencing. As you exhale—making a
slightly deeper exhalation than normal—allow what you are
feeling to fill you and grow. What do you notice? Did you
smile? Did you relax? Did you feel a warmth in your belly?
Did your vision soften, your eyes moisten with gratitude
for this precious item you are observing?

Attention is more powerful than most of us realize. The word comes from
Latin, meaning "to stretch toward." Philosopher and psychologist William
James defined attention as "the ability to hold something before the mind."
He added that attention brings us outside the self: "It's not just the other
that becomes real to us, but our attention itself that becomes palpable."[1] Da
Vinci's attention brought him well outside the self. It brought him to awe.

GRADIENTS OF ATTENTION

There are gradients of attention. We like to think of them as little *a*'s and
big *A*'s. Little *a* attention is mostly thoughtless. This is one of the miracles
of the mind—the ability to drive a car, have a conversation, and perform

many tasks without consciously focusing our attention on them. Most of us spend much of the day in little *a* because we live amid an overabundance of stimulation—phones, emails, pings, videos, televisions, schedules, long to-do lists—distractions of every kind. Too often, we don't choose what we pay attention to. We just react to a stimulus.

Big *A* attention has purpose. We set an intention to attend fully to something. Consciously focusing on one thing puts us in a state of readiness and receptivity. All our senses are poised for what is before us. To make the headspace for the object of our attention, we give up our random thoughts, distractions, and doing things on autopilot.

There's a gift in attending deeply to one thing even for just a few seconds. Attention gives us the space to see the object of our attention in a fresh way. We go deeper, beyond our preconceived thoughts, even to the point of fathoming the object's existence.

This creates novelty, or the cognitive accommodation that awe researchers talk about. To accommodate, or make room for our new perception, we change how we experience the object of our attention. This is how the emotion of awe unfolds. It's how Leonardo was able to see and then paint lips like no other.

Awe requires big *A* attention, and so to feel awe we need to pay attention to how deeply we attend to things—and what we're attending to.

RENDERING OUR REALITY

Jenny Odell, in her book *How to Do Nothing: Resisting the Attention Economy*, talks about how overwhelming it's become to decide what we give our attention to, given all the commercial entities vying for our attention—and our dollars. This invasion of our personal world is ceaseless and disruptive. For the most part, we're giving our attention to superficial things that really don't matter to us. And we have only so much to give.

Odell's message to disengage from the attention economy and "do nothing" coincides with a call to give our attention to what means something to us. And her message is urgent: "There are more reasons to deepen attention than simply resisting the attention economy. Those reasons have to do with the very real ways in which attention—what we pay attention to and what we do not—renders our reality in a very serious sense."[2]

We decide what to consciously attend to. The mess our partner leaves in the kitchen after making dinner can leave us feeling irritated all evening if that's all we see. Or we can focus on the delectable meal we were just graced with and enjoy cleaning the kitchen with some fun conversation.

We call this choosing "selective perception." What we choose to focus on—what we select to perceive—renders our reality in a big way, determining how we view and experience the world.

William James recognized how chaotic life would be if we didn't have this choice:

Millions of items of the outward order are present to my senses which never properly enter into my experience. Why? Because they have no interest for me. My experience is what I agree to attend to. Only those items which I notice shape my mind—without selective interest, experience is an utter chaos. Interest alone gives accent and emphasis, light and shade, background and foreground intelligible perspective, in a word. It varies in every creature, but without it the consciousness of every creature would be a gray chaotic indiscriminateness, impossible for us even to conceive.[3]

Selective perception is necessary and useful. Every second, millions of bits of incoming data bombard our nervous system—more information than we can possibly pay attention to. Without the ability to perceive selectively, our powerful yet underutilized and overstimulated brains would be overwhelmed. Selective perception also limits us for the same reason it keeps us functioning—it ensures we are aware of only a narrow slice of the world that surrounds us. The problem is that we don't consciously decide what not to attend to.

We may, for example, pay attention only to our needs and not the needs of others. We may focus on our pain and not our joy. We may see only our faults and not our strengths. We may pursue our goals with single-mindedness and never notice the weather or the birds chirping right outside the window. We may see what's wrong with our house and not what's charming. We may blindly accept and then rarely question a certain collective consciousness around race or politics or gender or the environment.

The result? We can stay stuck in the reality we've rendered without recognizing that it's based on only a thin slice of available data. Our beliefs and perspectives are limited and may even be holding us back. There's a much bigger world out there than we allow ourselves to notice.

AN A.W.E. MOMENT

To experience just a bit of what you might be missing, take time to look around your home as if you were in a museum, and stop long enough to appreciate some of the things you haven't recently paid attention to.

- Do you have a piece of art, a photograph that you can look at and appreciate?
- Do you have any sculptures, light fixtures, mirrors, or lamps that have a story behind them? Or a blanket, pillow, rug, perhaps a vase?
- When something captivates your attention, stop, wait, and breathe in slowly while giving your full attention to whatever you're looking at.
- Does it conjure any memories? Who gave it to you? What happened to them?
- How did you end up with this in your home? Notice its qualities, characteristics, and details and what you never noticed before. Exhale and expand into a smile.

Each one of these memories can provide a moment of awe, now that you take them in, one at a time.

TAKING SHORTCUTS

Another thing we do to ease some of the burden on our already busy brains is take shortcuts. Our brains have neurons dedicated to storing memories, and we take advantage of memories by using them to create assumptions and generalizations. This works quite well, especially for routine tasks. Every time we approach a door, for instance, we don't need to relearn what a doorknob is or how it works. We turn the knob and walk through. We don't have to give it a second thought because our brains have stored this data, even if we aren't conscious of it. It's as if our brains have a catalog full of preestablished ideas about our reality.

Taking shortcuts is, once again, necessary but limiting. Though these preconceptions help us manage the copious amounts of data coming at us every second, and though they are familiar and help orient us, they also plop us into a comfort zone of thoughtless disengagement. We go on autopilot, and in this state it's easy to take our world for granted. Not fully engaged with our environment—not being fully present—we miss much of the beauty and wonder that surrounds us. Before opening our front door, it's unlikely we stop to wonder how the doorknob works or was invented in the first place.

The brain's ability to use selective perception and then store some of that data for future use is brilliant because it ensures we'll make it through the day without "the gray chaotic indiscriminateness" William James refers to. We're able to make sense of our reality. But in the process of being selective, what are we missing?

A READY SOURCE OF AWE

Given that we realize only a nanofraction of our world, what if we picked one thing, one simple thing, and gave it some attention? So much of what surrounds us in the ordinary is worth seeing—or worth seeing with fresh eyes. Much of it is a ready source of awe.

Television personality Jason Silva is a firm believer in using the power of awe to exit autopilot. In his YouTube series called Shots of Awe, he eloquently describes how much we miss when disengaged:

I think a lot about the contrast between banality and wonder. Between disengagement and radiant ecstasy. Between being unaffected by the here and now and being absolutely ravished emotionally by it. And I think one of the problems for human beings is mental habits. Once we create a comfort zone, we rarely step outside of that comfort zone. . . . Overstimulation to the same kind of thing, the same stimuli, again and again and again, renders said stimuli invisible. Your brain has already mapped it in its own head, and you no longer literally have to be engaged in it. *We have eyes yet see not. Ears that hear not. And hearts that neither feel nor understand.*[4]

More often than we might realize, we can choose to inspire ourselves by escaping autopilot and re-rendering our reality, moving from the mundane to awe, or what Silva terms "radiant ecstasy." With A.W.E., we can decide to do that at any time and in only a few seconds. It starts by consciously giving our undivided attention to just a small piece of the beauty and wonder that surrounds us in the ordinary.

The A.W.E. Method hinges on giving big *A* attention to what we value, appreciate, or find amazing. This is the purpose of the *A* in A.W.E. Choosing to pay attention to things we *value, appreciate, or find amazing* focuses our mind and heart on what is likely to foster awe in the best sense of the definition.

When we're filled with awe, our sense of reality is altered. Things don't look the same anymore. Our preconception of the object of our attention has been ruptured, suspending any preestablished ideas we might have about it. This novelty creates a subtle disorientation. To adapt to this disorientation, we must accommodate our change in perception. This awakens our sense of wonder, and we step into a world tingling with endless and previously unforeseen possibilities. At this point, we aren't the same anymore.

This is the reality awe renders. Awe wakes us up to the extraordinary in what has become so very ordinary. Suddenly, a doorknob becomes a masterpiece of invention, a miracle. Everything around us takes on a spacious quality—a sense of timelessness and aliveness. And it all starts with attention.

Asking people to alter their reality by focusing on what is essentially something positive may sound trite, yet the domino effect is profound. Not only does this positivity lead to a positive expression of awe, temporarily altering and expanding our perception, but it is another reason why awe is good for our health and well-being. Positivity puts us in what's known in physics and medicine as *coherence*, a physiological phenomenon that's been studied extensively.

AN A.W.E. MOMENT

Consider that Osbourn Dorsey, a sixteen-year-old African American, submitted the first patent for the modern doorknob in 1878. The idea that a Black youth applied for and received a patent soon after the Civil War is awe filling in and of itself. But just less than two centuries later, we've taken him and the doorknob for granted. The notion that time has given the rest of us permission to forget about Dorsey and his accomplishment is also awe filling. For another awe-inspired moment, think of how the attention Dorsey gave to the simple act of opening and closing a door changed how the world forever enters a room or a closet.

COHERENCE: SURVIVAL OF THE HAPPIEST

Before Riccardo Chailly conducts Mozart's Symphony No. 40 in G minor, you can hear a pin drop. The theater is completely silent. Musicians are poised for the world-famous Italian conductor's hands to drop, signaling the music to begin. As the performers do their job, the music transports the audience.

Creating that magic requires that a lot of things go just so. All the instruments must be in tune, the musicians must be ready after having spent almost every day of their career either practicing or performing, the acoustics in the theater must be optimal, and the cymbals must clash at just the right moment. A magical symphony orchestra experience requires coherence. If even one component is off—if a trombone player blares the wrong note, for instance—it creates dissonance, and everyone in the music hall knows it. It's unsettling.

In the human body, coherence is a bit like a well-trained, highly disciplined symphony orchestra. In a state of coherence, all organ systems are working in concert with one another but also with the mind and emotions. When functioning as intended, the body does its job superbly. We can experience optimal blood pressure, reinforced immunity, deepened sleep, and more energy. In short, we feel good mentally, physically, emotionally, and spiritually—and we live longer.

As simple as it may sound, coherence is driven by electrical signals generated by the heart when we are feeling positive emotions. Love, enthusiasm, appreciation, joy, and awe can all bring us to a state of coherence in part by increasing heart rate variability (see Our Evolutionary Superpower: Connection in Chapter 3), which indicates that we are handling stress well. The HeartMath Institute has conducted numerous studies proving the relationship between feeling positive and being healthy.

It's worth noting, though, that awe stands apart from the other feel-good emotions. First, if we're depressed, we can't necessarily make ourselves happy in the moment, and so coherence is out of reach. Awe, however, is unique among positive emotions in that we can experience it even when depressed or experiencing other negative emotions. Second, using A.W.E., we can access awe immediately—in five to fifteen seconds—so that we don't have to wait until we are no longer feeling depressed to return to a state of coherence. A.W.E. is a quick path to coherence regardless of our emotional state.

Coherence isn't an all-or-nothing proposition. We are constantly adjusting—like an orchestra tuning its instruments—to try to return to some level of coherence. But when all is well emotionally—when we're

feeling positive—a healthy mind and body can maintain a high level of coherence. Introduce a stressful thought or experience—bring in the horn section too early, so to speak—and coherence is diminished.

The heart and brain are intricately connected, constantly exchanging neural signals. When we feel stress, a series of biological changes, including the
release of stress hormones, causes the heart to pump faster, and this change
in heartbeat directly affects the brain's emotional processes. Suddenly, when
under duress, we may find we can't think straight, can't remember what we
just read, can't make even simple decisions. We don't feel cheerful or loving.
We're on edge or even scared.

Stress disrupts coherence by switching on the sympathetic nervous system, the body's fight-flight response, and we enter into what is called "defense physiology." Now on guard, we're prepared with extra energy to defend
ourselves—or run away—from whatever we feel threatened by. The body is
functioning as it should. The sympathetic nervous system is supposed to kick
in when we feel threatened. But in this state, we are no longer experiencing a
high level of coherence. Threat cytokines (see Chapter 2) have been released.

For the longest time, science has taught that evolution designed the body
to be in the parasympathetic state most of the time so that the body would
have the energy it needs to function optimally, which would promote coherence. The stress response was just for emergencies. We've also been warned
that twenty-first-century stress is ongoing, not the occasional short-term encounter with a tiger or an invader that the sympathetic system was designed
to confront before returning to homeostasis. We've all heard it before: Most
of us stay in a state of stress for way too long. Our bodies are overtaxed by an
overactive sympathetic nervous system. We need to relax.

Some researchers have theorized that the optimal state of coherence takes
place in a "zone" of activation of the parasympathetic nervous system that
includes modest sympathetic arousal. Neither fully relaxed nor hyper on
guard, the body is instead stimulated and energized so that we're able to enjoy life or accomplish something. It's the energy we use to dance, make love,
sing in a choir, and connect with others. Researchers call this a mobilized, or
prosocial, state. This is also the state we enter when we experience awe.

One way to enter or return to coherence is by experiencing any positive emotion (such as awe or gratitude) for a brief period.[5] Under most circumstances, returning to coherence involves focusing on things or people that make us feel happy or grateful, for instance. This is perhaps why spiritual and self-help leaders tell us to be grateful and psychologists ask us to frame things in the positive rather than in the negative. But that's not always easy to do.

Darwin described an evolutionary process in which only the fittest in each species survived to pass on their robust DNA. Coherence shows us another side to the survival coin: survival of the happiest. Feeling positive emotions puts us in a healthy state physically and mentally.

Attention is the first step in accessing the emotion of awe, which is unique among positive emotions in that we can feel it in tandem with other emotions, even those we think of as negative. Awe puts the body in an optimal state of coherence, improving physical and mental health—which helps to explain why the A.W.E. Method worked so well in our study participants to reduce depression, anxiety, loneliness, burnout, and chronic pain and to increase well-being.

The next stage in the A.W.E. Method is the Wait—the pause when we enter what some consider to be the most sacred of all spaces—the present moment.

CHAPTER 5

W—WAIT: BECOMING PRESENT

The present moment is filled with joy and happiness. If you are attentive, you will see it.

—*Thich Nhat Hanh*, Peace Is Every Step: The
Path of Mindfulness in Everyday Life

Honoring the moment is honoring every human being you meet. The
only place where you can meet them is in the moment.

—*Eckhart Tolle*

If you recall, our definition of awe is "an emotional experience in which we sense *being in the presence of something* that transcends our normal perception of the world." The Wait in A.W.E. is the pause in which we experience presence—that quality of spaciousness where the mind isn't overthinking and processing but being an observer. With presence, there's no agenda. Nothing to do and no place to be. There's no thinking. Just being. Because we have chosen to be in the presence of something we value, appreciate, or find amazing, our experience of that moment is going to be nourishing and powerful.

But what enables the mind to pause and be present? And what happens when we aren't in the present moment? Where are we?

THE A.W.E. METHOD

Attention means focusing your full and undivided attention on something you appreciate, value, or find amazing. Look around the room you're in. Find that special beautiful something that you value and appreciate. Look at it closely. Really look. If it's a small object, pick it up and begin to notice everything about it. If it's a plant, touch the leaves; notice the texture, color, and smell; and notice the life inside it. If it's a painting, imagine the painter painting it and notice the depth, light, and colors.

Wait means *slowing down or pausing. So take a breath—inhale deeply while you appreciate this cherished item in your home.*

The final step, **Exhale and Expand**, amplifies whatever sensations you are experiencing. As you exhale—making a slightly deeper exhalation than normal—allow what you are feeling to fill you and grow. What do you notice? Did you smile? Did you relax? Did you feel a warmth in your belly? Did your vision soften, your eyes moisten with gratitude for this precious item you are observing?

THE DEFAULT MODE NETWORK

For decades, Marcus Raichle, MD, has worked to understand how the brain functions. Or in his words, "How does a piece of biology get itself organized?"[1]

Back in 2001, Dr. Raichle, as a neurologist at Washington University in St. Louis, used positron emission tomography (PET) and functional

MRI (fMRI) scans to compare the brains of two groups: subjects who were awake but doing nothing, and people focused on a task. What he found surprised him: In the control group of loungers, large areas of the brain lit up, indicating an abundance of neural activity. In the brains of the task-oriented individuals, activity in these same regions went dark. The conclusion? When we're not actively giving our attention to something—when we're not present—the brain automatically returns to a default mode, during which time some of our neural networks are shockingly busy.

Dubbed the default mode network (DMN), these regions of the brain, when active, are swimming with random thoughts or ruminations. The mind wanders from one thought to another, using stored data as fodder. We daydream, plan, worry, or think of how bored we are. We evaluate ourselves and consider how others see us. Here, we live in the stories we've created about ourselves. And we time travel, replaying memories and anticipating future events. We are anywhere but the present moment.

The DMN is the "monkey mind," the ongoing mental chatter most meditators seek to quiet. (Speaking of monkeys—chimpanzees and macaque monkeys also have a DMN, as do mice and rats.)[2]

To fuel these thoughts requires massive amounts of energy. Dr. Raichle estimates that the DMN metabolizes about 90 percent of the energy the brain requires. This is incredible when you think about it. And it seems a wasteful use of resources as well. Yet, for neuroscientists, this figure isn't surprising because the DMN is complicated. Though the DMN is not fully understood, Raichle and others credit it with a monumental task: keeping order in the brain by preventing competing brain signals from interfering with one another and "descend[ing] into anarchy."[3] So, although the DMN may be where we store some of the thoughts and perceptions that distract us, this network is an essential piece of biology.

In people whose self-talk is mostly negative, increased activity in the DMN has been linked to depression and anxiety. But the DMN is not always a place of negativity. It can be a happy place too.

Tor Wager, PhD, professor of neuroscience at Dartmouth College and a leader in brain imaging, is critical of how the DMN has been described by some scientists. He sees the DMN not as an actual network but as "a 'neural workspace' for representing concepts and thoughts related to the self."[4] According to Wager, quieting the DMN is less important than influencing its contents.

"I think of it more like a house than a volume knob or a switch," he wrote in an email to Jake. "[With a knob,] you can turn the volume knob down or up, but that's it. [A] house . . . can be a lot of things . . . it's what you put in it that is important."[5]

The DMN can be productive. It turns out that creativity might not transpire in the right side of the brain, as most of us have been taught to believe, but in the DMN. Creatives often refer to the workings of this space when they describe how ideas pop into mind upon awakening, on a walk, in the shower—when making pancakes—or when they're in the "doing nothing" state of mind that Jenny Odell talks about in her book. When the DMN is active, our musings can lead us to connect the dots and create something, even while sleeping, when the brain sorts through the day's new data and connects it with old memories.

So, a wandering mind can be useful—stumbling upon creative insights or solutions to problems. A wandering mind is also quite normal. Researchers say we spend at least half our days daydreaming, planning, or ruminating. Despite some of its advantages, a wandering mind does take us away from the present. And awe is in the present.*

To find awe, we need to briefly release the mind's wandering thoughts—whether creative, problem-solving, distracting, or otherwise—and quiet the DMN. Focused attention does this for us. This is why mindfulness practices are so popular and necessary. Every now and then, we need a break from the monkey-mind chatter, regardless of its content. We need to rest in presence.

Quieting the mind, or more specifically, the DMN, is a common goal in meditative practices, and meditation has also been shown to lessen negative self-talk and reduce activity in the DMN. But meditation takes effort. And

---

* When the DMN is less active and we become present, we don't necessarily forfeit creativity. When we reach a state of awe, a different kind of creativity arises—one born out of fresh perspectives.

some of us aren't very good at it. The fastest way to free our minds is to direct our attention to something we value, appreciate, or find amazing. Big *A* focus moves the mind from an idle state (which is when the DMN is most active) to an engaged state. When we concentrate on what we value, appreciate, or find amazing, we no longer hear the random and roaming thoughts in our head. This is the value of Wait.

TIME STANDS STILL IN AWE

The Patience of Ordinary Things
by Pat Schneider

It is a kind of love, is it not?
How the cup holds the tea,
How the chair stands sturdily and foursquare.
How the floor received the bottoms of shoes
Or toes. How soles of feet know
Where they're supposed to be.
I've been thinking about the patience
Of ordinary things, how clothes
Wait respectfully in closets
And soap dries quietly in the dish,
And towels drink the wet
From the skin of the back.
And the lovely repetition of stairs.
And what is more generous than a window?

Pat Schneider, *Another River: New and Collected Poems* (Amherst: Amherst Writers and Artists Press, 2005) p. 111. Reprinted with permission by the Estate of Pat Schneider.

The Wait phase of A.W.E. is also, we believe, when we experience an altered sense of time. There are three categories of time: past, present, future. The key to understanding how awe affects our relationship with time begins by understanding that awe brings us into the present. When the mind is present, the body releases dopamine, a neurotransmitter responsible for enhancing mood, reducing anxiety, and even acting as a pain reliever. Dopamine, in turn, has been shown to give us the sense that time is expanding—we feel like we have more time.

In studies in which people are given a dopaminergic drug (a drug that frees or activates dopamine), they perceive a minute of time in only thirty seconds. This is because more information is taken in every second, and thus the experience of time expands.[6] In turn, novel experiences elongate the minutes, making us feel as if we've been at a new place longer than we have been. Awe, as we know, invites us to experience the object of our attention in a novel way.

AN A.W.E. MOMENT

Recall a time when you were driving someplace you'd never been before on roads you'd never traveled. The journey to your destination may have seemed like it took forever. In contrast, traversing the same roads on the return trip likely went by much faster. The novelty of the journey on the way there affected your perception of time.

Michael intentionally used A.W.E. to, in effect, spend more time with his daughter. When she was a senior in high school, he became keenly aware that in the near future she would no longer be a part of his daily life. She'd be moving out to attend college. He couldn't stop that event from happening—nor did he want to. Rather, he had a profound moment of realization that this time with her was very precious. He wanted to prolong the time with his daughter, so he did just that. When he was with her, Michael used A.W.E. to alter his perception of time, making the moments he had with her richer, deeper, and more lasting:

As a mindfulness teacher, I was aware that craving for things to be different is a source of suffering. By clinging to the past, craving for time to slow down, and having an aversion to the inevitable changes in my future, I was creating more suffering. A.W.E. helped me to be fully present (attentive) and appreciative in each moment.

For instance, I would fully absorb myself in attending my daughter's water polo games and not get distracted by my cell phone, sad thoughts of this being her final season, or mindless chatter with other parents. I sat back in the stands in awe of my daughter's accomplishments, her skill, her beauty, and her grace in the water. I took in each moment: the reflection of light off the pool, the sounds of the crowds cheering, the sensation of the sun on my skin.

These forty-five-minute water polo games, which are fast paced, began to feel as if they lasted hours, as though time had slowed to a snail's pace. I was experiencing this time with my daughter profoundly and deeply. I also noticed my craving and aversion dissipate. I felt as though much of my life became a spiritual practice, not just on the cushion but out there in the world moment to moment. I had a deeper appreciation of how miraculous our lives were. We had blessings of peace, love, community, and opportunities of expansive connection and growth.

In the Wait phase of A.W.E., all we know is we're focused on something amazing, whether the squirrel outside our window, the sound of our partner's laugh, the fragrance of a zested lime, or our child playing water polo for the last time in high school. It's all we're aware of. We have no thoughts, just this awareness. While our awareness is full of what we are appreciating, we're inhaling naturally. We're taking in the beauty, and as we're taking it in, energy is building physiologically. Our heart rate is going up ever so slightly. And then we wait—just a slight pause—before exhaling.

THE GIFT OF WAITING

Have you ever experienced what it feels like when someone patiently, willingly, and intentionally waits for you? Waits to hold a door? Waits until you are finished speaking? Waits to speak until you are done crying? You feel attended to, recognized, even honored. Compare it to the feeling you have when someone makes any of these same gestures while looking at their watch. Their mind is in a different place and time, concerned about someone or something else, and you're left feeling unattended to or as if the gesture were ingenuine.

Waiting is a gift. You honor someone when you are willing to wait for them, to share a moment with them. It's a perfect opportunity to connect with another person, to honor the fact that you crossed paths at that moment. With the *W* in A.W.E., you are waiting for yourself. You are honoring your experience of being with yourself. It is a gift you can give yourself at any time.

Waiting, when done with intention, is one way to be fully present. And the gifts of being present are many. In *The Power of Now*, author Eckhart Tolle writes, "As soon as you honor the present moment, all unhappiness and struggle dissolve, and life begins to flow with joy and ease. When you act out of the present-moment awareness, whatever you do becomes imbued with a sense of quality, care, and love—even the most simple action." The flow and joy and ease that Eckhart Tolle says results from presence is none other than awe.

Presence creates the space for the emotion of awe—and the emotion of awe creates presence. When we're present, awe arises naturally. In that moment, we can flood the space with the novel, the unexpected—a bounty of possibilities we've never imagined. Now all we need is the *E*.

CHAPTER 6

E—EXHALE AND EXPAND: FINDING YOUR NERVOUS SYSTEM'S SWEET SPOT

For some people, the most potent part of A.W.E. is the exhale. There's good reason for this. Deep breathing can move our nervous system from the fight-flight state to the rest and repair state. Meditators who focus on taking deep breaths know this very well.

The physiology behind a good exhale is that it stimulates the vagus nerve, which in turn activates the parasympathetic nervous system. When a deep exhale activates the rest and repair state via the vagus, oxygen is diverted from the extremities (where it flowed to help us power a fight-flight move) to the brain. Our thinking sharpens as any stress we feel begins to wane. It has a relaxing effect.

This effect can be substantiated by what's known as the polyvagal theory—a nuanced way of looking at how the autonomic nervous system functions—and one way to help us pinpoint where awe arises within the ANS.

THE A.W.E. METHOD

Attention means focusing your full and undivided attention on something you appreciate, value, or find amazing. Look around the room you're in. Find that special beautiful something that you value and appreciate. Look at it closely. Really look. If it's a small object, pick it up and begin to notice everything about it. If it's a plant, touch the leaves; notice the texture, color, and smell; and notice the life inside it. If it's a painting, imagine the painter painting it and notice the depth, light, and colors.

Wait means slowing down or pausing. So take a breath—inhale deeply while you appreciate this cherished item in your home.

The final step, **Exhale and Expand**, *amplifies whatever sensations you are experiencing. As you exhale—making a slightly deeper exhalation than normal—allow what you are feeling to fill you and grow. What do you notice? Did you smile? Did you relax? Did you feel a warmth in your belly? Did your vision soften, your eyes moisten with gratitude for this precious item you are observing?*

JUST BREATHE

Much has been written about the importance of breath to health. When you breathe in through the nose and out through the nose, you create a different physiology than when you breathe in and out the mouth. The same is true if you take air in through the nose and out the mouth and vice versa. Slow versus rapid, long versus short, shallow versus deep. How we breathe can affect snoring, allergies, sleep apnea, and even how straight our teeth are, as well as our emotional state.

It's all incredibly fascinating. But we want you to forget about it.

When practicing A.W.E., we want you to breathe more or less as you normally do—with just a slightly longer than normal exhalation—without thinking about it. The key to A.W.E. is to experience the benefit of the full respiratory cycle while focusing on something you value. Your practice will become so immediate that you won't be thinking about the A.W.E. steps, much less how you breathe. Thinking about the steps, in fact, takes you out of awe.

THE POLYVAGAL THEORY: A NUANCED LOOK AT THE AUTONOMIC NERVOUS SYSTEM

Although we can consciously use breathing techniques to calm the nervous system, the ANS is by definition automatic and operates unconsciously, in effect forcing the lungs to breathe, the heart to beat, and adrenaline to pulse through the body when we're frightened—all functions necessary for survival and best not left to choice.

Most of us learned the traditional view of the ANS in middle school biology class: The ANS comprises two branches: the sympathetic nervous system (fight-flight-freeze) and the parasympathetic nervous system (rest and repair). The brain activates these two systems depending on how we perceive—often unconsciously—what is going on in our environment. The ANS effectively scans our environment for us and interprets any signs of threat.

Since 1994, Stephen Porges has been challenging parts of this accepted truth with the polyvagal theory, which suggests that the parasympathetic nervous system itself (the rest and repair portion of the ANS) comprises two very distinct branches: a ventral vagal system and a dorsal vagal system, both of which stem from the vagus nerve—ventral (front) and dorsal (back). By including the ventral and dorsal vagus nerves as part of the parasympathetic nervous system, the PVT offers a more nuanced way of understanding some of our behaviors and responses.

For instance, have you ever entered a room full of people and either knew you were welcome or sensed you didn't belong? This ability to instantly read a room is hardwired into our nervous system, which acts as a kind of internal bodyguard, letting us know when we're safe and alerting us when we're not. How we respond to this room full of people depends on what our nervous system is telling us. Porges explains that there's a hierarchy of ANS responses that enable us to be socially engaged, mobilized, or immobilized.

Optimally, we will feel socially engaged. This state is the mother of all safety responses. When around people who greet us with open arms, smiles, and genuine warmth and caring through their words, actions, and tone of voice, we feel calm and comfortable. And we're able to communicate extremely effectively. Social engagement is possible when our ventral vagus nerve is activated.

Now, let's say we spot an old friend in the room who we're in conflict with. We're anticipating conflict—an interaction that will not give us a feeling of calm and safety—and the nervous system tells the body to release hormones such as adrenaline and cortisol. On a dime, we shift from social engagement to mobilization. This mobilized state activates the sympathetic nervous system, or fight-flight. We feel anxious, and the level of tension builds as our physiological state changes.

If we engage with that person in our mobilized state, we might raise our voice in anger, or in the most extreme circumstances use our fists or run out of the room to escape the tension. Mobilization is not bad, but it can get us into trouble if we show inappropriate aggression. When used appropriately, mobilization helps us be productive, play, set boundaries, and refuse to do something unreasonable, for instance.

If the situation ramps up and the tension further increases, mobilization may no longer be helpful. At this point we might reach a state of immobilization and "freeze." We may not be able to speak or move. If the body is physiologically overwhelmed—say, our blood pressure reaches a deadly level—the nervous system activates the dorsal vagal response, and we might faint. This response occurs only when we perceive cues of extreme threat. We have no control over this response.

People freeze for a variety of reasons when they perceive a threat. Being verbally attacked or physically abandoned are just a couple of examples. An anesthesiologist we know told us she sees some patients shutting down in this way—immobilizing—prior to surgery.

UNFREEZING

When we freeze, we eventually have to mobilize again. We can do this by rebooting the body-brain connection through body awareness—nodding our head, moving our eyes, paying attention to our senses. Birds go through a similar process. After hitting a window, they shake. Experiencing awe is another way to mobilize.

Porges's model of the nervous system offers a clear explanation of why we behave the way we do at times. It also gives us a framework for the unique way that awe activates the ANS. Awe brings us into the social engagement state that is predominantly relaxation with some extra juice from the sympathetic nervous system.

In an excerpt from an email to Jake, Dr. Porges describes it this way:

Awe would maintain the calming effect of the vagal influences, while providing an "appropriate" energizing of the sympathetic nervous system, while keeping the sympathetic system "constrained" outside of a mobilized defensive state of aggression/anxiety/fight/flight. Hypothetically, you would see more playfulness and spontaneous social engagement following awe than following meditation.[1]

Another way to think about nervous system responses is to consider threat and safety cytokines (see Chapter 2). When our bodies produce safety cytokines, we're more likely to be socially engaged in a healthy way. When our bodies produce threat cytokines, we're more likely to be aggressive or to withdraw or collapse. Awe is a quick way to increase safety cytokines, helping us shift into a healthier place from which we can more easily relate to others.

Feeling safe and socially engaged is also a way of being in the present moment. When we reach the *E* phase of A.W.E., we are already fully present—feeling utterly safe and unstressed. A deep exhale stimulates the ventral vagus nerve, enhancing vagal tone (which we learned in Chapter 3 is good for our health!) and fully activating the body's social engagement system. Not only are we feeling safe and relaxed, but we also feel more inclined to connect with others.

The fastest way to feel safe when there is no imminent threat is to enter the present moment—and awe is one way of doing so. Our ancestors seemed to have figured this out.

CONTEMPLATIVE NEUROSCIENCE

Recent research reveals that our ancestors understood the benefits of activating the ventral vagus nerve, even if they hadn't named it and didn't fully understand its functions. It turns out there's physiology behind the ancient practices of chanting, meditating, and praying.

Dr. Porges's study of the physiology of ancient rituals and the vagal tone that results during these practices has led to a new discipline called contemplative neuroscience.

Chanting, for instance, activates the ventral vagus nerve in the throat, and sustaining a chant requires long exhales and deep abdominal inhales. It's no accident that this same breathing pattern is part of most meditation practices because it helps create a healthy vagal tone. And prayer? The posture—kneeling with hands clasped before us—affects the carotid baroreceptors, the body's blood pressure sensors, which help the vagus regulate blood pressure.

The benefits of stimulating the vagus nerve go beyond health. Dr. Porges contends that the neural pathways affected by the vagus can promote calmness and stillness and "enable expansive subjective experiences related to compassion and a universal connectedness."[2] Sounds a bit like awe.

We place A.W.E. into the contemplative neuroscience bucket. As of this writing, plans are underway to look at how A.W.E. can be used as a medical intervention to help COVID-19 long haulers and patients who have suffered heart failure. These upcoming studies at UC Davis will determine the efficacy of the A.W.E method in circumstances where no other treatment thus far has been effective.

Interestingly, enhancing vagal tone has a domino effect that leads to what we call the Three Cs.

THE THREE CS: COREGULATION, CONNECTION, AND COHERENCE

A healthy ventral vagal tone not only motivates us to connect with others but also leaves us *better able* to connect because of a condition known in therapy circles as *coregulation*.

Coregulation occurs when one person's nervous system is soothed by another person's nervous system. When someone is "losing it," or feeling overwhelmed or discombobulated, for instance, they are in what's known as a dysregulated state. Being in the presence of someone who is warm, calm, and caring—characterized by a specific tone of voice, kind facial expressions, and helpful verbal acknowledgment—can soothe and mitigate distressing emotions. The person with the agitated nervous system "attunes" to the person with the well-regulated nervous system, and the result is coregulation.

We like to think of coregulation as sharing a healthy ventral vagal tone with someone who needs it. Therapists are trained to coregulate with clients. In psychotherapy, it's widely accepted that the quality of the relationship a client has with the therapist is one of the most important elements, if not the most important element, in influencing the effectiveness of treatment.

We have all been with someone who is good at coregulation. We feel more relaxed and comfortable in their presence. Jake has extensive training in coregulation and perhaps a natural propensity for it. One day, for example, he visited a client's workplace to give him a book. Jake sat in the waiting room until his client was done with an appointment. When his client came out of his office, Jake smiled, and the client said, "Seeing you sitting here is just as good as having a therapy session." In that moment, the two connected and coregulated. Coregulation can be that quick.

Coregulation can calm another's nervous system. Emotionally, as stress and anxiety dissipate, the person begins to feel more positive. If the body returns to homeostasis, the person can enter coherence, that healthy state when all systems—thoughts, feelings, energetics, intentions, and behaviors—are aligned. In this light, it's easy to see how coregulation leads to connection, as many studies have shown, and positive connection opens the door to coherence, which leads to greater well-being and longevity.

As an emotion, awe is unique in its ability to align the Three Cs. One of the most remarkable things about awe is that it allows coregulation–connection–coherence to happen when we are with other people *and* when we are alone. When we are alone and access awe, we coregulate with something beyond our ordinary self—maybe it's nature, our higher self, God, the Universe, or humankind—and connecting with that "source" leads to a state of coherence that facilitates wellness and healing.

AN A.W.E. MOMENT

Try standing up, loosening your shoulders, and settling into a relaxed stance. With eyes open or closed, think of someone in your life who is a source of coregulation for you—they help you relax. This person could even be deceased. Now think of a time when being in their presence helped you calm down. Picture the setting, think of the conversation (if any), and recall how you felt in this person's presence. What about this person made you appreciate them so much? Now inhale that appreciation. Allow the energy to fill your body. As you exhale, become conscious of your spine. Of the energy running up and out your spine. Some people feel a chill or a tingle as the energy expands.

The A.W.E. Method is not the only way to arrive at this unique physiological destination. But A.W.E. is the fastest, most direct way we're aware of. A.W.E. resets our nervous system by shifting us, quickly, into a ventral vagal state. Now we are poised to Expand.

THE EXPANSION

Real joy means immediate expansion. If we experience pure joy, immediately our heart expands. We feel that we are flying in the divine freedom-sky. The entire length and breadth of the world becomes ours, not for us to rule over, but as an expansion of our consciousness. We become reality and vastness.

—Sri Chinmoy, The Wings of Joy: Finding Your Path to Inner Peace

We talked about building energy during the inhale, which happens during Wait. When we exhale, we release the energy, stimulate the ventral vagus, and feel a sense of calm and safety. As we relax, the sensations embodied during the inhale do something significant—they expand.

Some people feel the energy move up the spine and out the body. This release, sometimes experienced as a chill or goose bumps, is none other than a release of nervous system energy that was previously constricted.

For some people, the exhale and release can be a moment of disorientation. It's a brief and simple moment. Sometimes the shift is subtle and might be described as a "pause" in our consciousness. Other times it's more pronounced and makes us go "wow, something happened." In this moment there's not only a physiological shift but also a psychological shift. Our energy shifts, our nervous system rests, and we come back different. It can be that quick and simple.

> At the beginning of the pandemic, the A.W.E. practice helped a lot. There was no sense of control, and my world narrowed during lockdown. I felt isolated. The A.W.E. Method helped create a sense of peace, and each time I practiced it I felt a greater sense of the world around me. It expands my whole sense of myself when I practice. It helps create a broader sense of the world and gets me out of any narrow focus I may be having about life, the world, catastrophe.[3]
>
> —Jennifer

While disoriented, we've no way to frame or define what we're experiencing—no preconceptions to rely on—and so we experience cognitive accommodation. It's the moment Jason Silva talks about when he says, "One of the ways that we elicit wonder is by scrambling the self temporarily so that the world can seep in."[4] In this instant, we are receiving new data, fresh perspectives. The world, seen through the eyes of awe, is seeping in.

In a TED Talk, University of Sussex neuroscientist Anil Seth gives us a neurological explanation for how we accommodate a new perspective. Although he's not speaking about awe, his experiment with an audio recording is an awe moment in and of itself.

Imagine you're a brain. You're locked inside a bony skull trying to figure out what's out there in the world. There's no light inside the skull. There's no sound either. All you've got to go on are the streams of electrical impulses, which are only indirectly related to things in the world, whatever they may be. So perception, figuring out what's there, has to be a process of informed guesswork, in which the brain combines the sensory signals with its prior expectations or beliefs about the way the world is to form its best guess of what caused those signals. . . . What we perceive is [our brain's] best guess of what's out there in the world.[5]

To illustrate changes in perception, Dr. Seth played—at a very high speed—an incomprehensible recording of someone speaking. He then played a slowed-down version so we could easily decipher the words. He then re-played the high-speed recording. Remarkably, the high-speed recording was now completely discernible. Dr. Seth describes what happened this way:

The sensory information coming into the brain hasn't changed at all. All that's changed is your brain's best guess of the causes of that sensory infor-mation and that changes what you consciously hear. . . . Instead of percep-tion depending largely on signals coming into the brain from the outside world, it depends as much, if not more, on perceptual predictions flowing in the opposite direction. We don't just passively perceive the world, we ac-tively generate it. The world we experience comes as much if not more from the inside out as from the outside in.[6]

Every time we experience awe when focusing on something we value, appreciate, or find amazing and alter our perception, we actively generate an awe-filled perception of the world. In *The Wondering Brain*, Kelly Bulkeley describes it this way:

To feel wonder is to experience a sudden *decentering* of the self. Facing some-thing surprisingly new and unexpectedly powerful, one's ordinary sense of personal identity is dramatically altered, leading to new knowledge and un-derstanding that ultimately *recenter* the self. The profound impact of this de-centering and recentering process is evident in both the intense memorability of the experiences and the strong bodily sensations that often accompany them. People speak of being stunned, dazed, breathtaken, overwhelmed, consumed, astonished—all gesturing toward a mode of experience that ex-ceeds ordinary language and thought and yet inspires a yearning to explore, understand, and learn. This is where the noun "wonder" transforms into the verb "to wonder," where the powerful emotional experience stimulates lively curiosity, knowledge-seeking behavior, and critical questioning: "And it makes me wonder. . . . "

The decentering of the self that comes as we wonder in awe and open to new perspectives leads to ego dissolution, or the small self. Paradoxically, as our ego gets smaller, our identity has room to expand.

THE EXPANDING IDENTITY

Although it sounds counterintuitive, expanding your identity is essentially the same as dissolving your ego. We prefer to describe it as a process of expansion versus dissolution because expansion supports the idea of integration. We are not getting rid of some parts of ourselves—ego—we are growing and expanding beyond our previous sense of self.

Developmental psychologist Erik Erikson defined identity as a "fundamental organizing principle which develops constantly throughout the lifespan."[7] Identity is a mental construct, an internal experience of "I am," applied to our life roles, gender, race, ethnicity, status, disabilities, abilities, religion, values, and behaviors. Identity is autobiographical.

Identity is built out of memories and expectations—accomplishments, failures, family dynamics, significant relationships, hopes, and aspirations—and is expressed as part of our narrative. *My mother abandoned me, and that's why I haven't been able to have close romantic partners in my life. I'm afraid of being hurt again.* There is no absolute that says if you were abandoned by your mother, you will be unable to have a close romantic partnership. Such beliefs are interpretations—one way of making meaning of an interpersonal dynamic between parent and child. Holding on too tightly to stories that we use to build our identity can be limiting. Most aspects of our identity are highly flexible, and they change over time if we allow them to.

Other aspects of our identity are fixed. We may be Hispanic, Jewish, Asian, an immigrant, or have a physical disability. Those descriptors may be accurate and unchanging. That's indisputable, but our ideas and interpretations of even those descriptors can change and evolve, and as they do, our identity evolves.

We spend the first couple decades of our lives forming our identity—determining our values, deciding what kind of people to be and to befriend, considering our talents and where we fit in. Being adventurous, an environmentalist, an intellectual, a spiritual seeker, a loner, a risk taker—these are examples of behaviors, labels, and beliefs that can be part of an identity.

A healthy identity gives us a sense of stability, security, and continuity that is helpful in an ever-changing world. When we get up every morning, if we have a clear sense of who we are and how we conduct ourselves as we go into the world, this helps quell anxiety.

However, challenges to our identity can lead to anxiety because our identity is central to who we think we are. It's important to us. Too often, when we feel as though someone is challenging our identity, we become anxious, and our sympathetic nervous system activates. For example, if someone tells us we're wrong or that they no longer like us or if they make fun of us, we may mobilize and react as if we were being *physically* threatened. We defend ourselves—arguing (fighting) or walking away (fleeing) or immobilizing (freezing). But none of these reactions to the perceived source of our anxiety is useful because we are usually the true source, and it doesn't help to fight with ourselves, run from ourselves, or freeze ourselves.

There's a difference between fear and anxiety. Fear is a response to a specific, immediate danger. Anxiety is a response to something we anticipate happening based on our interpretation of events. Anxiety can be addressed in what's known as a top-down approach, using our prefrontal cortex, the part of our brain that creates meaning. With practice, we can learn ways to alter meaning, such as by using the A.W.E. Method or changing the way we use language, which we explore in Chapter 8. Anxiety can also be addressed in a bottom-up approach, which involves becoming aware of bodily sensations and movement.

Interestingly, the A.W.E. Method activates both top-down and bottom-up benefits. It can produce cognitive accommodation that allows us to alter the meaning we are making of an event, and it can carry us beyond words by stimulating our senses.

Either way, top-down or bottom-up, awe is an effective way to reduce anxiety that arises when we feel as though our identity is being challenged. The first step is realizing that *threats to our identity are not threats to our survival.*

By realizing that identity is self-determined—we choose how we define ourselves—we can become less reactive to judgments and criticisms. As we relax our attachment and fixed ideas about identity, we are likely to feel more spaciousness, as if we have stepped out of an outfit that is restrictive or too small. Stepping out can feel like a relief, an opening to fresh possibilities. Our identity becomes porous—like a mesh that allows potential and possibilities to seep in. It might suddenly occur to us that we do not fit a stereotype or that we could do something out of our comfort zone: hike Denali, paint a portrait, make a banana cream pie, or simply not react when someone questions our worth.

Nietzsche once said that whatever doesn't kill us makes us stronger. We believe he was talking about identity. If a challenge doesn't kill us, it most likely strengthens and expands our identity.

This discussion is separate from ones we might have about threats to our identity that can lead to physical violence—violence based on race or sexual orientation, for instance. If we identify as gay and are verbally attacked because we are gay, we may very well be under physical threat, and it's appropriate that our fight-flight response activate. Being bullied for being shy or not fitting in is another example. A known history of such attacks is central to our reaction in these cases.

Instead, this discussion of overreacting to threats against our identity centers on events that are unlikely to lead to violence but that create a strong defense within us nonetheless. Most of the time, especially when interacting with people we are close to, it helps to remember that threats to our identity are not threats to our survival.

Expanding our identity is valuable and necessary for a full life: The more it expands, the more we can identify with other people, and the more capacity we have to connect with them. As a young adult, for instance, we might not have been able to empathize with somebody who was ill because we had no clue what it meant to be feeble; we didn't relate to their experience. Likewise, we may not know how to relate to people who are going through loss. But if we personally go through these experiences or feel compassion for someone who is going through them, our identity expands. Gradually, a porous and expanding identity makes us more unique, complex, and resilient individuals.

Awe creates a greater porosity of identity (ego). In a Simulation: Global Enlightenment interview, author Michael Pollan refers to the dissolution of the ego and the idea of an expanding identity that occurs when the default mode network goes quiet, which happens when we experience awe:

> Without a sense of time, you don't have a sense of identity. . . . So how interesting that when [the default mode network] goes quiet, or appears to on an fMRI, that's when people report an experience of complete ego dissolution. . . . When the default mode network goes down, all these new connections form that have never existed before. The brain is temporarily rewired and suddenly you have this explosion of new pathways, and we don't know what's happening on those pathways.[8]

• • •

We think of awe as a neuronal lubricant that facilitates the rewiring, making it easier for us to glide into different states of consciousness. And we believe that the primary task of the modern brain is to elevate our consciousness and expand identity. Expansion is the trajectory of our evolutionary timeline. Our expansion happens as we go beyond the familiar and open to new perspectives and experiences, and it results from the culmination of physiological and psychological changes triggered by three simple steps: Attention, Wait, Exhale and Expand. A.W.E., then, is a doorway to profound presence, spaciousness, ease, and peace—a fast track to transcendence.

PART III

A.W.E. AND THE FUTURE OF MINDFULNESS

CHAPTER 7

WHAT IS MINDFULNESS, ANYWAY?

Dacher Keltner at UC Berkeley refers to the A.W.E. Method as "the future of mindfulness" because such a short, effective mindfulness practice you can do anywhere appeals to people who feel as though they don't have the time to establish a formal mindfulness practice. The world, after all, has changed a lot since people started practicing mindfulness long, long ago. And mindfulness practices are changing with it.

Twenty years ago, when Hannah, Jake's wife, would attend retreats in Zen meditation (a form of mindfulness), she'd go away for seven days and sit in meditation for eight hours a day. She was not allowed to talk except when she met with the Rōshi, the Zen master, to answer a *koan*—a riddle of sorts. These highly regimented sessions were meant to foster focused discipline, which quiets the mind. These formal sessions were also incredible, sometimes life-changing, experiences. But not everyone could take the time to do them, much less devote hours every week to meditating. Consequently, the number of people practicing meditation was limited.

Today, many mindfulness practices are much less structured. People use apps on their phones or weave mindfulness into day-to-day activities, such as mindfully washing the dishes, gardening, or walking. Over the last several decades, some of the most ancient mindfulness practices have morphed into very simplified versions of their former selves and have been given secular or even clinical names: mindfulness-based stress reduction, mindful self-compassion, and mindfulness-based cognitive therapy. This is part of the evolution of mindfulness.

This move from formal to informal is why more people now have the time to practice mindfulness. In the United States alone, the percentage of people who have at least tried meditation jumped by 10 percent between 2012 and 2017 to about thirty-five million adults and children.[1]

Whereas those Zen meditation retreats fall at the formal end of the spectrum, A.W.E. sits at the opposite end. It's about as informal and approachable as mindfulness gets.

MINDFULNESS: BEGINNING IN THE EAST

Mindfulness is an umbrella term for numerous practices, many of which originated in the East, in Hinduism and Buddhism, thousands of years ago. Meditation is one form of mindfulness; yoga, tai chi, and qigong are some other examples. They all require a certain amount of discipline, a bit of training, and a time commitment. Reaping the benefits of these formal practices requires first acquiring the skills and then committing to the discipline.

But being mindful can be done, too, through simple acts—such as by giving your full attention to whatever you are doing. It can also be a little more complicated—such as learning the moves to a Sufi dance.

Types of Mindfulness Practices

Concentration practices (word, thought, sensation, image): Transcendental Meditation, Vipassana (body scanning), prayer, chanting/mantra repetition, mandala

Movement-based: Yogi, tai chi, qigong, Sufi dancing

Cultivating positive emotions (compassion, forgiveness, gratitude, loving-kindness): Buddhist metta, tonglen, HeartMath Institute training (gratitude and compassion)

Emptying practices: big sky meditation, centering prayer

Secular mindfulness: mindfulness-based stress reduction with various exercises including breath awareness, body scan, object meditation, walking meditation, eating meditation, mindful stretching

How we choose to enter a higher state of awareness is personal and sometimes cultural. Most people gravitate toward what suits their personality. Perhaps they enjoy gaining the physical strength associated with yoga or are adept at a meditative religious or spiritual practice they learned in childhood, such as tai chi.

The means is not important. A talented whirling dervish on stage is just as capable of reaching transcendence as a nun reciting the Hail Mary in a pew. But if we have two left feet and can only sit still comfortably for minutes at a time, neither Sufi dancing nor the Rosary is likely to take us to the "end," or to the spaciousness we wish to experience.

The simplest definition of mindfulness is being fully present in and accepting of the moment. As with the *A* in the A.W.E. Method, we do this by giving our full attention to what we are doing or witnessing. With an open and curious mind, we can turn what is routine into an awakening experience. When drinking a cup of tea, for instance, we notice the feel of the cup. As we take a sip, we become curious about our beverage's temperature. If it's lukewarm, we just accept that. There's no judgment. Immersed in the moment, we're just a witness to the experience. Replacing judgment with acceptance quiets the mind.

As we become an observer of our experience, we increase our awareness of what we're experiencing. We might, for instance, hear our internal monkey-mind chatter (some of that default mode network activity) judging our lukewarm tea. But when mindful, we observe our internal judgments, let them go, and refocus our attention.

Mindfulness works to different degrees for millions of people and can lead to more awareness, presence, and a calmer state of mind. It can also give us powerful insights, helping us connect with the hidden insights of our subconscious or something greater than ourselves. With enough practice, mindfulness can lead to a heightened state of consciousness—what we like to call spaciousness.

A COMMON THREAD

Mindfulness is often recognized as a spiritual practice on par with awe and religion. Although spirituality, awe, and religion have certain differences, they are linked by a common thread: they are a means of connecting to something greater than the self, and they can all lead to the small self.

In an analysis of the personal stories in the book *Awakening to Awe*, a collection of interviews with people who've experienced awe, researchers extracted ten themes from the stories. One of them was that people felt as if they were in the presence of something holy—"a transcendent presence of some sort."[2]

In a Zoom interview with us, Kirk Schneider, psychologist and author of *Awakening to Awe*, offered the following about where awe fits in as a spiritual practice: "A sense of awe captures that dynamic tension between our mortal, vulnerable selves and our more godlike transcendence. And it seems to me that that's where a lot of the juice is—in terms of creativity [and] in terms of evolving and growing as people and being on the edge of inquiry."[3]

One major goal of mindfulness is to reduce suffering—especially the mental anguish we might take on when something happens that we don't like (such as divorce) or when our default mode network is overactive or filled with negative content. In *Neurodharma*, neuropsychologist and mindfulness expert Rick Hanson writes, "The sense of being a self causes a lot of suffering, including taking things personally, becoming defensive, and getting possessive. When the sense of self decreases, well-being usually increases, with a feeling of ease and openness. As Anam Thubten put it: no self, no problem." This is the small self, or the dissolving ego, we talked about earlier. Like the emotion of awe, mindfulness practices can lead to the small self.

BRINGING MINDFULNESS TO THE WEST

For some people, *Jon Kabat-Zinn* and *mindfulness* are synonymous. Kabat-Zinn, a professor of medicine, author, and founder of the Stress Reduction Clinic and the Center for Mindfulness in Medicine, Health Care, and Society at the University of Massachusetts Medical School, studied Zen Buddhism in the East before becoming one of the first people to bring a secularized version of it to the West. He called his less formal program mindfulness-based stress reduction (MBSR), and in the 1970s he began teaching it to people to help reduce stress, anxiety, depression, and pain. The eight-week program, which incorporates various mindfulness practices and also looks at cognitive behaviors, is still used widely in hospitals and other settings.

THE CHALLENGES OF MINDFULNESS

As teachers and lifelong practitioners of various mindfulness practices, we are well versed in their benefits, which include reducing stress, anxiety, and depression and improving stress-induced medical conditions such as irritable bowel syndrome and post-traumatic stress disorder—many of the same benefits associated with A.W.E.

We are also familiar with the limitations of some mindfulness practices in today's busy world: the pressure to spend twenty to thirty minutes a day meditating, the effort it takes to bring oneself to the present moment, the self-judgment that comes with missing a session or that may surface when comparing one's practice with others'. For many people, the rewards of mindfulness have not been fully realized because traditional mindfulness and meditation are hard to sustain. As beneficial as they can be, they lead to transcendence only for a minority of practitioners, usually those who not only are highly disciplined but also able to focus for long periods of time. Michael is a good example.

After having a panic attack while taking the Medical College Admission Test, Michael committed to learning and practicing mindfulness to keep his mind healthy for the long journey ahead to becoming a doctor. His first meditation retreat was a ten-day silent Vipassana course. Michael recalls how challenging it was both physically and emotionally to do the hour-long meditations for fifteen hours a day. His body was in pain from sitting so many hours, and during the silence, his mind chatter only amplified. In some ways, the meditation retreat was more challenging than the academic and physical demands of medical school.

Michael persevered with a lot of willpower and over time developed a lasting meditation practice that included attending several retreats a year and participating in a regular weekly meditation group. In his late thirties, his mentors at Spirit Rock Meditation Center nominated him to become a teacher, and he commenced a two-year training program. Afterward, Michael started and led an interfaith meditation group and has since taught meditation to hundreds of his patients in group mindfulness programs for chronic pain.

Despite being immersed in the world of meditation, it took twenty years of practice before Michael finally had his first moment of profound transcendence—the same sense of spaciousness that people routinely experience within seconds using the A.W.E. Method.

Many people find that trying to be mindful, or focusing on the present moment and practicing acceptance, is hard to do throughout the day. They can practice for moments at a time, but when they get a ping on their phone or start thinking about their to-do list, the practice is interrupted before it's begun. They get distracted before they have a chance to experience the benefits of a higher level of consciousness.

For some people, including those who are highly auditory and those who struggle with depression, traditional meditation can have unintended consequences, such as negative internal self-talk. Individuals with a trauma history might experience flashbacks, stress reactivity, and dissociation as a result of traditional meditation practices.[4]

Physical mindfulness practices—such as yoga, qigong, and Sufi dancing—may be difficult for people who are ill or physically disabled. Sitting meditation can be uncomfortable. It's hard to get present if we're thinking about our sore joints and aching backs and wondering when the ending bell is going to ring.

Because it's so quick and easy, the A.W.E. Method sidesteps these problems. But there is much more that sets A.W.E. apart from other mindfulness practices.

A BRIEF RESET: BEGINNING AT THE END

When we spoke to Rick Hanson about our A.W.E. Method and asked how he thought it fit into the mindfulness bucket, he had much to say. He summed up A.W.E. "as a brief intervention that resets people" and described the A.W.E. Method as "profound":

Under our nose all along has been this extraordinary power that we each have over the course of a handful of seconds to reset our whole stress chemistry, to reset our brain and pull up and out of stressful contraction into an authentic appreciation of what is actually real right around us that we can dwell in, if only for a few seconds, and come out refreshed, stronger, clearer, more open-hearted, and more effective.

For thousands of years, humans have looked up to the stars, marveled at the birth of their child. They have appreciated the vastness around them. And now modern science is revealing the hidden power of awe in everyday life, which we need now more than ever, as so many forces around us pull our attention close because we feel threatened, pressed, and "stressed" thin.

Hanson sees A.W.E. as having some common ground with mindfulness and departing from it in some subtle ways.

One of the wonderful things is that while doing this very simple A.W.E. practice, you are getting multiple bonus benefits including developing greater mindfulness while expanding your appreciation of the good that is also true in and around you. This is a great way to train in mindfulness. Many people find traditional mindfulness training practices relatively un-stimulating and thus hard to sustain. Becoming more mindful by spending more time in a state of grateful awe is a lovely, powerful way to strengthen steadiness of mind.[5]

And, unlike the original form of mindfulness, A.W.E. is not neutral. We ask people to focus on something they value, appreciate, or find amazing. A.W.E. encourages us to start with a positive slant.

However, one thing sets A.W.E. apart the most, perhaps. People on a personal growth or spiritual path usually expect that "someday" they will experience greater ease and more love, compassion, and acceptance. They ex-pect that this transformation will take many months and years of dedicated practice to achieve—just as Michael experienced. A.W.E. turns this idea upside down. Using the A.W.E. Method, we can experience these qualities right now, in this moment. In doing so, the journey is no longer about some future destination. It's here and now in the present.

Instead of waiting for the end of the journey, which for many people in-volves years of disciplined meditation, we can start at the end and reap the benefits now.

This is possible, in part, because A.W.E. is not a behavior change. It doesn't bump up against what traditionally prevents people from making changes in their lives—including fear of failure, fear of success, procrastination, and lack of time. The list goes on.

In *Atomic Habits*, author James Clear argues that a habit requires a cue (information that predicts a reward), a craving (motivation), a response (habit), and a reward (something pleasurable). He and other experts help us understand that focusing on reward-based behavior change is far more effective than relying on willpower. Juddson Brewer, MD, PhD, author of *The Craving Mind* and *Unwinding Anxiety*, has developed many successful mindfulness programs that focus on intrinsic rewards over willpower when treating addictions. A.W.E. accomplishes what Clear and Brewer are talking about, but A.W.E. delivers a reward instantly.

A.W.E. can be done anywhere, even in full public view on a crowded train, in the checkout line at the grocery store, or while picking the kids up from school. Although others might sense that your energy has shifted and even pick up on your good vibes, the people around you are otherwise none the wiser.

> The A.W.E. practice has improved my life by helping me to slow down. I love that I can practice it when others can't even tell. There will be a moment when I feel like either myself or others are going a mile a minute. All I have to do is bring my attention to something, wait a moment, and exhale deeply. The awe practice is accessible anytime, anywhere. It calms my nervous system and provides greater ease in my body and my life.[6]
>
> —Jennifer

People who have a hard time meditating or being mindful, as well as those short on time, may prefer A.W.E., which leaves no time for distractions or negative self-talk to interfere. As with mindfulness, a phone call, for instance, can interrupt a feeling of awe. But we can usually return to it as quickly as we left it. And there's a cumulative effect. The more we practice A.W.E., the more spontaneous our awe moments become. It's as if we are, with little effort, forming a new habit that rather likes itself. At some point, we find we don't need to invite awe. It just shows up, unannounced, like a very welcome guest.

A.W.E. is not better than any other avenue to transcendence, but—for most people—it's certainly faster and easier because it's done in microdoses. We've found that A.W.E. appeals to meditators and nonmeditators alike because the shift happens so quickly.

But A.W.E. is more than just a shortcut. It's a clinically proven process. We, Jake and Michael, have spent decades following meditation regimens, attending meditation retreats, and teaching mindfulness classes. Although we were able to transcend many of our daily frustrations for moments at a time, we never experienced transcendence to the level we do now—and certainly never on a moment's notice.

We encourage meditators and practitioners of yoga, qigong, and other disciplines to continue doing what they enjoy while trying A.W.E. at least three times a day. It can even be fun to buddy with a partner or community of A.W.E. practitioners to share moments of awe and deepen the experience. We'll touch on that more in Chapter 11.

Adopting A.W.E. as a practice changes the context of life. The same effect transpires through other mindfulness practices. But with A.W.E., the results are similar or even greater because we're encouraging a positive state. In billiard terms, A.W.E. puts a little English on mindfulness practices, which tend to be emotionally neutral.

About now, you might be wondering: *If awe is in the everyday and so accessible, why don't we experience it more often naturally?* Part of the reason awe doesn't come naturally to some people is that their sympathetic nervous system is in overdrive more often than is necessary. Many of us don't feel safe enough to open up to awe. But we have a solution for this.

CHAPTER 8

HOW SPUTNIK LAUNCHED A NEW TREATMENT FOR ANXIETY

O n October 4, 1957, the Soviets launched Sputnik, the world's first artificial satellite, into orbit, marking the beginning of the Space Age. Technologically, the satellite was a source of awe in the best sense of the definition, traveling eighteen thousand miles per hour and orbiting Earth every ninety-six minutes. For Americans, however, the satellite was a source of anxiety. Sputnik, US scientists and military leaders understood, could be easily positioned to launch a nuclear attack against the United States.

At the time, the Soviet Union and United States were a dozen years into the Cold War, a conflict and rivalry that involved an arms race, space race, and polar political and ideological beliefs. Both nations had nuclear weapons and the know-how to produce more. In the eyes of the public in both nations, the cost of losing the Cold War was certain annihilation.

A feature article in the January 13, 1958, issue of *LIFE* magazine, "Citizens Give Ideas in Crisis," reported on a meeting convened to address steps necessary to counter Soviet scientific advances. Attendees included some of the best and brightest in their respective fields: Henry Kissinger, who would later become secretary of state; Paul Nitze, who would serve as US deputy secretary of defense; Ernest O. Lawrence, a nuclear scientist and winner of the Nobel Prize in Physics; Father Theodore Hesburgh, president of the University of Notre Dame; and many more. Also among them was John Weir, a lesser-known yet highly respected doctorate-level psychologist.

What were a priest and a psychologist doing at a meeting about the arms race? They were there to explore ways to lower the nation's anxiety levels.

The Soviets' launch of Sputnik heightened anxiety levels across a nation already weary of war and fearful of the spread of Communism. The experts at this meeting were there to talk about solutions, and they came up with several, including increased funding for scientists, the military, and math and science programs in high schools. They recommended building missiles, fallout shelters, and communication systems for civil defense. This kind of action could ameliorate some concern by enabling the nation to be better prepared should the Soviets attack and by deterring an attack in the first place. But short of requiring everyone to build an at-home fallout shelter stocked with nonperishable food, what could be done to relieve the nation's angst?

As far as we know, the meeting produced no immediate psychological answers for anxiety-ridden Americans, but it did spur John Weir, along with his wife, Joyce, to develop a method individuals could use to lower their personal angst—to calm their nervous system and help them feel safe. This method centered on what is to each of us very personal: our perceptions.

PERCEPTION: HOW CAN WE ALL BE RIGHT?

The brilliant physicist John Wheeler—who coined the term "black hole" and played a vital role in the Manhattan Project* (code name for the research

---

* The Manhattan Project began shortly after Albert Einstein learned that the Nazis had split the uranium atom—creating enough energy to power an atomic bomb—and shared the news with US president Franklin Roosevelt to warn him. Although many people associate Einstein with the development of the atomic bomb, he was not among the scientists who participated in the Manhattan Project. When Einstein learned that an atomic bomb had been dropped on Hiroshima, Japan, in 1945, he is reported to have said, "Woe is me" ("The Manhattan Project," American Museum of Natural History, https://www.amnh.org/exhibitions/einstein/peace-and-war/the-manhattan-project).

and development of the first atomic bomb) and later the design and development of the hydrogen bomb—said, "There is no out there out there—we are all observers in the universe—it's a miracle that we construct the same vision of it."[1]

Like many of the experts we quote in Chapter 4, Wheeler understood that we do not really know the world outside ourselves but create it based on *how we make meaning* of our perceptions. This is what renders our reality. In an article about Wheeler, one journalist summed it up this way: "To Wheeler and others, we are not simply bystanders on a cosmic stage; we are shapers and creators living in a participatory universe."[2]

That same journalist referred to Wheeler "as having one of the most adventurous minds in physics." As Wheeler liked to say, "If you haven't found something strange during the day it hasn't been much of a day."[3]

John Weir, likewise, had one of the most adventurous minds in psychology. He and Joyce thought that the key to helping people move through anxiety was to give them a greater sense of personal empowerment, or self-responsibility. The Weirs achieved this through a linguistic model they developed called Perception Language, or Percept.

JOHN AND JOYCE WEIR

John Weir was a professor of psychology and a contemporary of Rollo May, Carl Rogers, and Abraham Maslow—all leaders in the human potential movement that arose in the 1960s. This movement was about helping people reach their full potential, which was new and cutting-edge at the time.

Joyce emigrated from Australia with her parents as a young girl. She became a professional artist and worked as an animator for early cartoon studios in Hollywood (she

(continues)

> (continued)
>
> drew Betty Boop and Popeye). She was a dancer, trained in body movement and somatic expression, and was gifted at finding ways to connect the body to the psyche.

Percept turns how we typically converse inside out. Its goal is to convey that we are talking about our perceptions of the world, not the world. It is based on the idea that any one person's perception of an event is different from another's perception of the same event. Communicating about something as if both parties have the same perception often leads to confusion, conflict—and anxiety. This linguistic model empowers us while reducing confusion, conflict, and anxiety.

The Weirs created Percept to address the inescapable truth that "there is no out there out there." As Wheeler recognized, it is a miracle we all construct a similar version of reality—that we identify a bus as a bus, a cloud as a cloud, a doorknob as a doorknob. Each of us interprets the world subjectively yet talks about people and events as if our interpretations were objective—as if they were the only perspective. When we have different subjective interpretations—different perspectives—how can we both be right?

In applying this model, the Weirs broke with some long-standing views, including the stimulus–response model, which was—and still is—a cornerstone of psychology.

THE SPACE BETWEEN STIMULUS AND RESPONSE

In 2004, author Stephen Covey wrote a foreword[4] in which he said, "In 1969, I took a sabbatical from my university teaching to write a book. Wandering through the stacks of a university library in Hawaii one day, I pulled down a book, opened it, and read three lines that truly changed my life.

They became the foundation for my own work, *The 7 Habits of Highly Effective People*. Here are the lines:

> Between stimulus and response there is a space.
> In that space lies your freedom and power to choose your response.
> In those responses lie your growth and your happiness.*

Covey's bibliomancy (and moment of awe) led to a best-selling book and a business empire. And it all centered on a basic tenet of psychology—the gap between stimulus and response.

There are many different schools of psychology, and almost all of them accept the idea that there is a world out there acting upon us. Someone or something (a stimulus) is doing something to us, to which we have a response. Someone tells us we're wrong, and we get defensive. Someone flirts with our partner, and we get jealous. A car cuts us off, and we get mad. Someone interrupts us, and we snap back.

Leaders in the field of psychology have attributed our responses to a variety of sources: the unconscious (Freud), learned behaviors (B. F. Skinner), levels of development (Maslow), or distorted thinking (Beck). A shared goal of most psychological models is to help people develop better responses to events (stimuli). We're encouraged to explore the unconscious and our childhood, process our feelings, reexamine our beliefs, learn new behaviors, learn to self-soothe, look at our patterns of relationships, empower ourselves by increasing ego strength and level of development, and change distorted thinking.

As we discussed in Chapter 2, even our physiology is understood to work according to stimulus and response. Our body is exposed to some type of foreign body, and our immune system reacts. As organisms, we're in a

---

* The quote Covey cites has often been attributed to Viktor Frankl, but according to the Viktor Frankl Institut, "The true origin of the quotation is somewhat involved." When asked, Stephen Covey said he couldn't remember the name of the book he pulled off the shelf that day, nor its author ("Alleged Quote," Victor Frankl Institut, https://www.univie.ac.at/logotherapy/quote_stimulus.html).

milieu, a constancy of stimuli, and we're responding all the time. Sometimes consciously but most of the time we're doing it unconsciously.

The Weirs recognized the limitations of the stimulus–response model. First, the model leads some people to unnecessarily enter a state of mind where they believe they are a victim—they feel as though the stimulus is doing something to them—which can be disempowering. Second, most therapy addresses people's behavior and beliefs after the fact—while they are sitting in a therapy session and recalling what happened. Third, therapy based on this model can go on forever. The daily barrage of incoming stimuli never stops, so people feel overwhelmed or worn out always trying to find better ways to cope and respond to the world. Participating in this type of therapy can be exhausting.

The Weirs shifted the focus from finding better ways to respond to the stimuli to considering how people make meaning of a stimulus in real time, during the gap. The goal was to help people realize two points:

1. They are making meaning of the stimulus based on their state of mind, unconscious biases, and memories of previous experiences to form a subjective interpretation or perception.
2. They can change the meaning of their interpretation or perception by changing the way they talk about it.

The primary way we make meaning is through language, and the Weirs understood that if we change how we talk about something—if we phrase it so that we fully understand and acknowledge that we are expressing only *our perception* of a stimulus—we become more flexible, curious, and less attached to being right and making others wrong.

Because it involves some novel concepts and, initially, some awkward syntax, Percept requires the speaker to slow down, which brings them into the present and creates curiosity instead of conflict when people have different beliefs, needs, wants, values, and experiences. By default, Perception Language requires us to be responsible for how we think, feel, and act, which is empowering and creates a sense of safety. But Percept does something more.

By keeping us in the present and self-reflective for just a bit longer than usual, Percept increases the space between the stimulus and the response. It gives us more of what Covey found so inspirational—choice. Our response to a stimulus is more measured and thought-out than reactive, so we tend to make better choices.

PERCEPTION LANGUAGE

Perception Language, like awe, is novel and requires cognitive accommodation—a different way of seeing and making sense of ourselves and the world. Following are some of the highlights of Perception Language, all of which are pretty simple to master:

- As much as possible, talk about what's happening in the present moment.
- Remove blame and praise from every conversation.
- Understand that we are the source of our feelings.

It sounds a bit out of the ordinary, and it is. But those who learn and use Perception Language often make a distinction about their lives "before Percept and after Percept." This model creates a turning point in their relationships and how they view the world, in part because it alleviates copious amounts of anxiety. Ultimately, Percept helps people (metaphorically) separate their nervous systems from one another—to disentangle them—which is useful when they're around someone who's anxious, upset, or judging them.

Keep the conversation in the present. So many spiritual teachers talk about being in the present and yet don't offer pragmatic ways for how to do it. The Weirs said that if you want to be in the present when interacting with others, talk about what's happening right now, what you need right now, what you want right now, or what you can do for someone in this moment. There's no point, in other words, of arguing about whether you said you'd be home by six o'clock (which is what you remember) when the other person remembers something very different. Those conversations are unproductive.

The question is, What can I do now—in this moment—given that we don't agree on when I was supposed to be home? That brings the conversation to a productive place and breaks the cycle in which people fight to be right. The present moment is the one in which we can make changes, regardless of who said what when.

Remove blame and praise. If you take away blame, you decrease anxiety levels dramatically. So much of our anxiety stems from projecting the idea that other people are being critical or judgmental of us. As soon as I blame you, you're likely to feel threatened. When I blame you, I'm telling you about you. I'm not telling you about my experience. But when using Perception Language, the speaker tells you about *their* experience, which decreases the tendency of the listener to get defensive. For example, instead of telling a person, "You ruined my day because you didn't give me a birthday present" using Percept, the speaker would say, "I disappoint myself because I didn't get a birthday present from you."

And Perception Language removes praise, as well, because when I praise you, it's as if I have control over your nervous system: if my praising becomes the source of you feeling pretty good about yourself, I can stop praising you and take that good feeling away from you.

Instead of praise: "You're so wonderful. You are a brilliant writer," Percept uses the word *appreciate.* "I appreciate having you in my life." "I appreciate how moved I feel when I read your poems." "I appreciate that you get your homework done before playing games with your friends."

Understand that we are the source of our feelings. This piece of Perception Language is based on the idea that our feelings come from us, not other people. We are responsible for our emotional life. But in our culture, we tend to say things like "You make me so angry." We blame others for our feelings, which means that, if we are to be soothed, we need the other party to stop making us angry. This happens in therapeutic settings as well. The most common question therapists ask their clients, for instance, is "How did *that/he/she* make you feel?" This reinforces the idea that the external event, or another person, is causing us to feel the way we do.

By changing our language, we challenge the perpetrator–victim model. It's no longer the case that you are making me feel the way I feel. Stepping out of that model gives me a lot more control over—and responsibility for—how I feel. For example, *I get so frustrated when you come home late from work* becomes *I frustrate myself when you come home late from work. You make me feel unimportant when you don't call* becomes *I make myself feel unimportant when you don't call. Your tone of voice is intimidating* becomes *I intimidate myself with your tone of voice.* For more examples of Percept, visit ThePower OfAwe.com.

AN A.W.E. MOMENT

Think of a situation that is troubling you, perhaps an ongoing source of frustration between you and a loved one or something about which you tend to feel insecure. Now try talking about it using Percept and see how different you feel. You can say the words out loud to someone or say them to yourself. Do you feel more empowered? Does Percept change how you might handle a situation?

Ginger has studied and learned Percept from Jake and Hannah. Here's how she describes its value:

One of the most significant and permanent shifts in my life came about when I became "fluent" in Perception Language. In my first few coaching sessions with Jake, he introduced me to the concept of Perception Language, and I began to incorporate it during my sessions with him. As we worked together, it became clear to me that my perceptions of my life and the roles I played in my relationships were skewed, painful, and one-sided. I saw myself as a victim and blamed others for my angst and deep loneliness.

I was estranged, by choice, from two family members and didn't have a solution other than compromising myself by returning to unhealthy ways of relating. And the guilt I felt regarding my son and my inability to be a good mother appeared to be not only unforgiveable but impossible to rectify. The wreckage of my past and the pain I had caused felt insurmountable to me.

I had made attempts in the past to "fix" my relationships, but my solutions required that all three of them agree with me that I was a victim of abuse and therefore not entirely responsible for my behavior—as a sister, a cousin, and a mother. It wasn't until I started using Perception Language that I began to take responsibility for all my actions, regardless of my history.

Changing how I spoke changed how I thought. That in combination with the principle of "no praise and no blame" helped me to see that I was the author of my story and could change not only my attitudes and behaviors in the present, but I could also change how I thought about the past. I empowered myself with the new language. And that enabled me to own my mistakes and relate with people, in particular these three, from a place of honesty and integrity.

How I related with these three as an adult had nothing to do with my abusive childhood. What occurred when I was a toddler was not a valid excuse for me to be jealous, submissive, or absent.

When I reconnected with my brother, I was his sixty-two-year-old sister—a mature, kind, and loving adult. We embraced being together in the moment and all the animosity and jealousy melted away in our happiness of being reunited.

I was able to tell my cousin how I had hurt and confused myself as a young woman when he behaved inappropriately, and I made it clear that I would no longer tolerate his abusive behavior and that I wanted to end our connection.

And when I truthfully apologized to my son and accepted responsibility for my neglectful and hurtful behavior, he forgave me and invited me to be a member of his family and a grandmother to his children.

In each of these conversations with my family members I changed my way of relating with them. I now relate with my brother and son as a woman of honesty, integrity, love, joy. I no longer approach them as a guilty or resentful person. I am clear about who I am and live according to my values, and they see that and respect me. In the past my words and actions did not match up—I would say I was sorry and then continue with the same poor behavior.

I also changed how I relate with myself. My conversations in my head and with others no longer focus on problems and lack. Perception Language and the A.W.E. practice have changed what I look for in life. Where I used to see pain, struggle, and conflict, I now look for joy, possibilities, and connection.

The practice of microdosing awe is something I continue to do on a daily basis, and the rewards are immediate, effective, and have changed my approach to life. Perception Language has changed how I think and how I communicate, and the freedom and the joy that I experience by being an honest and mature adult are invaluable.[5]

Frequently, we act as if someone else is running our nervous system. Severing that cord removes a great deal of threat from interpersonal dynamics. When on the receiving end of Percept, we're less likely to feel threatened or as if we're being accused of something, and our autonomic nervous system doesn't mobilize before we even have a chance to think about what's happening to us. Instead, we experience the calming effect produced by the ventral vagus nerve. From here, we're better able to respond calmly, think straight, and pause to consider how we make meaning of the stimulus, and perhaps even come up with a solution to whatever problem we're having. The idea that a long-standing argument we've had with a partner can be resolved in a few minutes by reconciling perceptions is powerful stuff.

When on the sending end of Percept—when we're the speaker—we slow down, become more present, and communicate intentionally. We stop blaming others and stop victimizing ourselves. We are less concerned about what other people think of us, and better able to represent ourselves. As we take complete responsibility for how we make meaning of whatever experience we're having, we empower ourselves. Guilt and regret decrease while acceptance and self-respect increase.

When both parties use this model, it becomes easier to hear and understand each other. But even when one person uses Percept, life gets easier.

A RADICAL INSTRUMENT WHOSE TIME HAS COME

Perception Language never took off as a widely adopted model of communication—but it continues to offer great promise. An article written in 2006 describes the Weirs' work as revolutionary: "No human development theorist-practitioner from the 1960s to the present has created as radical and powerful an instrument of personal authenticity, accountability, and self-empowerment as the Weirs' percept language. Moreover . . . no theorist-practitioner has placed personal responsibility for one's own development so firmly at the core of their personal growth work as did the Weirs." [6]

FROM PERCEPT TO AWE

By taking the threat out of interactions, Percept helps us feel safe and socially engaged. To practice A.W.E., we do need to feel some degree of safety. It'd be impossible, for instance, to do the A.W.E. Method while being chased by a tiger. The brain simply won't allow it because it's too busy trying to keep us alive. And by the way, "tiger" is a metaphor for extremely frightening situations—whatever that might be for a person.

Removing the threatening tone from a conversation is central to keeping the fight-flight system at bay and leaving us feeling safe enough to experience awe. In turn, by becoming socially engaged, curious, and more willing to accept a different perspective, awe helps us resolve even long-standing conflicts.

Walt, one of Jake's clients, uses Percept to approach events with curiosity and to go deeper into awe.

> Increasing awe in my life is less about seeking it and more about reorienting my attitude, interactions, and stories to deepen awareness of my surroundings and connections. When that deepening happens, I experience more awe. By inverting the stimulus–response model, Percept fosters accountability. Having more agency (in situations, in relationships, with myself) helps create space for richer appreciation of just about anything: expansive horizons, warmth from holding hands, hearing a hummingbird's wings, or hearing nothing. All of which I have awed myself with.[7]

John and Joyce Weir refined their model over a period of forty years, teaching it as part of the curriculum in group therapy retreats they offered. Most of their work was done at National Training Labs in Bethel, Maine. Human resource professionals and corporate executives attended these "labs," or places to experiment, to develop better leadership and communication skills. But the Weirs also traveled around the country—in their twenty-four-foot Winnebago—conducting smaller retreats for people interested in a group therapy experience. Their group therapy and encounter groups were on the leading edge of the humanistic psychology movement.

Carl Rogers, another prominent psychologist, hailed these types of early encounter groups as "the most rapidly spreading social invention of the century, and probably the most potent." Rogers went on to explain:

> I believe it is a hunger for something the person does not find in his work environment, in his church, certainly not in his school or college, and sadly enough, not even in modern family life. It is a hunger for relationships which are close and real; in which feelings and emotions can be spontaneously expressed without first being carefully censored or bottled up; where deep experiences—disappointments and joy—can be shared; where new ways of behaving can be risked and tried out; where, in a word, he approaches the state where all is known and all accepted, and thus further growth becomes possible.[8]

PALI: A VERBING LANGUAGE

Although Percept was unique at the time the Weirs introduced it, it has at least one precedent. Pali, the language that the Buddha spoke during his lifetime, was a "verbing" language. It allowed one to stay in process, not fixing oneself or clinging to a static or permanent state but rather being in motion. This creates a continuous unfolding of our awareness of self. Everything is in motion—evolving and unfolding all the time.

That nothing is static is a foundational premise of Buddhism. For example, nirvana, Buddhism's practice goal, would not be a noun but a verb—"nirvana-ing" ourselves: (actively) putting out our fires of greed, hatred, and delusion rather than reaching a state of nirvana. Instead of the Buddha finding a path to enlightenment (a static state), he would say that he was finding a path for enlightening ourselves—an active, continuous process.

Maybe because the "verbing" language was so radically different, significant numbers of Buddha's followers were waking up to the idea that "self" was a process, dependent upon one's interpretations and responses to conditions arising and passing away.

BREAKING THE GLASS CEILING

In 1998 the Weirs and Jake and Hannah Eagle met for the first time. The Eagles studied with the Weirs for six years and eventually became stewards of the Weirs' body of work. This changed the way Jake approached clients in his private practice, and just as John and Joyce had done, Jake and Hannah began offering weeklong labs (retreats) for people interested in personal growth. They saw results similar to what the Weirs had found: People felt empowered and less anxious. And their relationships improved.

After about a decade, Jake and Hannah noticed a pattern: Perception Language works when we're using it, but the tendency for many people is to return to their defense physiology. To help people break free of this pattern, the Eagles created a new model called the Three Levels of Consciousness.

The Weirs helped people shift their attention to an earlier stage in the stimulus–response model. People learned to notice how they were making meaning of stimuli in real time—and they understood they had a choice about how to interpret whatever it was that just happened. With the Three Levels of Consciousness, the Eagles took this a step further. They suggested that if people choose and practice being in a more resourceful state of mind *before* a stimulus ever arises, they will respond appropriately instead of being reactive.

So, what are the Three Levels of Consciousness, and how do we choose the most appropriate level?

CHAPTER 9

THE THREE LEVELS OF CONSCIOUSNESS

Have you ever wondered why one day you feel inspired to flip off the person who cut you off in traffic while another day you simply hit the brakes and then go your merry way as if nothing happened? The same event elicits different responses at different times because you are in different levels of consciousness at different times.

Throughout this book, we've mentioned that A.W.E. takes us to a higher level of consciousness. But what does that mean, exactly? *Consciousness* is not some abstract concept. It's our state of mind—our thoughts and feelings at any given moment. We're going to introduce you to a model that focuses on three levels, which we call Safety, Heart, and Spacious—the Three Levels of Consciousness, or the 3LC.

The 3LC model suggests the state of consciousness we are in will always influence how we perceive a situation, the choices we see for ourselves, and our actions. In other words, it affects *everything*.

Jake and Hannah developed the 3LC model more than a decade ago to help clients improve how they responded to external circumstances, or stimuli. Instead of working with people at the level of consciousness they were in when they presented their problems or concerns, Jake would help them shift their level, which consistently resulted in new perspectives and choices. Having the ability to shift their level of consciousness—at will—empowered clients. Jake's approach was a fresh take on an old problem—how to get people to change reactions that aren't useful and to do so without endless self-reflection and introspection.

The 3LC has proven to be a game changer. The approach eliminates the need to resolve many problems that exist at one level of consciousness because they dissolve when we shift to another level. A project we've put off for weeks becomes surprisingly easy to start. The tone of a long-standing argument we've had with our partner shifts so that the conversation and outcome are refreshingly different from what they were in the past. We stop worrying so much about what others are thinking about us. Moving to another level of consciousness doesn't eliminate all problems, but it can give us a fresh perspective. Life's problems feel less burdensome and more distant, and we might feel we have more choices.

SUBTLE SHIFTS TOWARD EMPOWERMENT

Poverty, abuse, neglect, social injustice, certain physical and emotional challenges—these serious problems may seem beyond amelioration. A shift in consciousness may not solve such problems, but shifting consciousness is an act of personal empowerment that creates movement, and when people are stuck, movement is helpful. The A.W.E. Method is an easy way to create movement.

Most of us don't know what level of consciousness we're in at any given moment, and why would we? People ask us how we are, not what level of consciousness we're in. But the 3LC model makes it easy to identify our level of consciousness. It's kind of like a mindfulness road map, with a big red arrow labeled "You Are Here" that points to where we are and another arrow that shows us the direction we might wish to take given the circumstances.

Learning to consider levels of consciousness can even complement or accelerate traditional therapy for conditions such as depression and anxiety. And it completely alters the process of couple's therapy. Conversely, being in the "wrong" level at the wrong time or for too long can be exhausting and lead to chronic anxiety, fatigue, depression, and for couples, a lack of intimacy.

In this chapter, we explain how to easily identify your level of consciousness and give you tools—including A.W.E.—to shift from one level to another. We show you how to break the glass ceiling that keeps many of us from accessing our full capacity for joy, connection, and inner tranquility.

First, we're going to describe each level of consciousness—Safety, Heart, and Spacious—so that you can confidently answer what might seem like an esoteric question: What's your level of consciousness? We'll start with Safety, which is where we spend most of our time.

Three Levels of Consciousness

Spacious · AWE · Expansive / Nonverbal / Nontemporal

Heart · Appreciation / Gratitude

Safety · Reward · Purposeful • Proactive • Productive
Safety · Stuck · Anxiety • Anguish • Ambivalence
Safety · Threat · Fight • Flight • Freeze

SAFETY CONSCIOUSNESS

Safety Consciousness is the state that most of us wake in each morning, perhaps reciting a laundry list of what we need to accomplish or face during the day. We also access Safety Consciousness when we feel fear, anxiety, or stress—conditions that signal that we need to take action, something isn't right, or we are under some kind of threat. Every day we receive many invitations to enter Safety Consciousness: we get an upsetting phone call, an overdraft notice arrives in the mail, or we need to meet a looming deadline.

Some of the time, we don't feel as if we have control over whether we're in Safety because it's driven by the amygdala, the more primitive part of the brain that can hijack our consciousness when we feel threatened. Yet, most of the time, we have more control than we might think.

Safety Consciousness can be divided into three degrees: Reward, Stuck, and Threat (see the figure on page 129). Some of us know Safety–Reward as "good stress." We're energized by the need to take care of business, learn a skill, or socialize. So Safety can be a highly productive state. It is what the polyvagal theory (see Chapter 6) would refer to as a mobilized, prosocial, even playful state. Maybe we're learning a new script for a community play, getting ready for a first date or audition, or excited to meet people we've never met before.

Safety–Stuck is a less welcome yet typical state for many people. Here, our life isn't in mortal danger but, faced with a divorce, a problem at work, or a health concern—anything we interpret as a problem—we may feel stuck. This can show up as ambivalence, uncertainty, confusion, varying degrees of depression, or anxiety.

And then there's Safety–Threat, which most of us know as the fight-flight-freeze response. We perceive that we are in a physically life-threatening situation. To save ourselves, we instinctually fight, flee, or freeze.

The purpose of Safety Consciousness, regardless of which degree we're in, is ultimately to keep us safe. Being productive (Reward) ensures we take care of business, care for our possessions, and care for our health. Feeling confused or ambivalent (Stuck) can give us time to integrate thoughts and emotions, which hopefully leads us to action. Freezing, fighting, or fleeing (Threat) when we encounter a life-threatening situation can save our lives.

For instance, Jake recalls working with a married couple who were forced to close their small bookstore because they couldn't compete with the big chains and Amazon. Lianne and Paul were both in their midsixties and had planned to keep working for another ten years, and from a financial perspective, they needed to. As soon as Lianne sensed that her livelihood was threatened, she started looking for another job. She was motivated, proactive, and productive. She contacted her network, created a résumé, and filled out applications. Being proactive helped minimize the anxiety she was feeling because the idea of being unemployed made her feel unsafe—how would they pay their mortgage?

Paul's response was entirely different. The perceived threat of no longer being his own boss was overwhelming to him. He couldn't stand the idea of working for someone, being told what to do, and being judged for his performance. He saw himself as a victim. What was happening was not of his doing and felt unfair. Who could have predicted the demise of independent neighborhood bookstores? Seeing no good alternative, Paul felt utterly stuck. He'd been making a good living. Who was going to match his salary? Who was even going to hire a sixty-five-year-old man who had worked for himself for what seemed like forever? Paul became depressed and anxious. Eventually, his anxiety turned to anguish.

While Lianne was using all her skills to ensure she would still feel safe, Paul had some emotions to work through before he felt comfortable moving on. It took him another six months of being stuck before he accepted that he had to take a lower-paying job for a while. Each of them was driven by a need to feel safe. Paul hindered himself with his anxiety, whereas Lianne put hers to good use.

We live in a world of endless stimulation, and we respond to most of it from Safety Consciousness, which activates our sympathetic nervous system. That can be useful, as it was for Lianne, or it can lead to chronic anxiety, fatigue, and depression, as happened to Paul.

Navigating the Reward and Stuck levels of Safety Consciousness requires certain skills: listening, planning, preparing, critical thinking, patience, objectivity, open-mindedness, curiosity. But even people who have these skills can get stuck. No matter how well we manage ourselves in Safety Consciousness, we all need to expand our consciousness from time to time. The easiest way to begin is to enter Heart Consciousness.

EXPANDING FROM SAFETY-STUCK INTO HEART

Can you wiggle your fingers? Can you wiggle your toes? Waggle your tongue? Do you appreciate that you can do that? Not everybody can. How do you feel when you realize you have the ability to wiggle and use your toes and fingers and waggle your tongue? That realization opens the window into Heart Consciousness and can free you from feeling stuck. Heart is a wonderful way to open yourself.

HEART CONSCIOUSNESS

Look at everything as if you were seeing it for the first or last time. Then your time on earth will be filled with glory.

—Betty Smith

Heart Consciousness is familiar to most everyone. Think of moments of delight, occasions when a friend was there for you, or a time when you were there for someone. All these situations give rise to appreciation, which is at the heart of Heart Consciousness. Appreciation transpires in simple pleasures or moments of profound relief. The HeartMath Institute and others have compiled at least twenty years of research that supports the health benefits of appreciation and gratitude, including decreased depression, better immune response, improved sleep, and even reduced inflammation—all attributed to the physiological state of coherence (see Coherence: Survival of the Happiest in Chapter 4).

Regardless of the circumstances, when we access Heart Consciousness we experience a physiological and psychological shift that alters the way we see the world and the way others see us. Others can tell we're in Heart Consciousness because communication feels light and natural. We are relaxed, giving, and loving. We realize how much we have to be grateful for, even if things aren't exactly as we'd like them to be. Often, gratitude carries us beyond ourselves, especially when we feel grateful to someone or something other than ourselves, which might be nature, another person or community, or God.

Heart Consciousness is not simply a state of positivity. It's not something that results only from a good day or a good situation. We can feel appreciative even when in pain. When Jake had an accident and cut his forehead open, Hannah took him to the hospital to get stitches. During the ordeal, he experienced Heart Consciousness while he was appreciating Hannah, the hospital staff who helped him, and the technology that made it all possible.

Gratitude requires appreciation of at least some aspects of a situation. In a difficult interaction with another person, maybe we can appreciate the intentions of the other person or simply their companionship. Opportunities for appreciation are ongoing. Looking for them is the path into Heart Consciousness.

For most people, Heart Consciousness is easy to access. We did it as children without thinking about it. It's a choice to see things through a heartfelt lens, and one way to access it is by a verbal expression—simply saying "I'm grateful," "Oh, that's magnificent," "I appreciate you," or "I feel so fortunate." A palpable shift takes place when we appreciate something or someone, and the feeling amplifies when we express our appreciation. Many people feel energetic movement within their chest, in the area of the heart.

Heart Consciousness is essential to our nature. Its purpose is twofold: to help us self-soothe and to help us connect with others. Moving into this level of consciousness balances the nervous system and decreases anxiety. Worrisome thoughts dissipate, replaced by gratitude and appreciation.

Feeling judgmental is a good opportunity to practice moving into Heart Consciousness. When judging someone, try imagining that person's perspective and assuming they have positive intentions. This exercise is more difficult to do in Safety, when we feel guarded and cautious. But in Heart, we can feel enlightened.

Michael, for example, was in the process of buying a new home in an area he'd always wanted to live, but after his offer was accepted, it didn't go well. When it came down to how much it would cost to buy some of the furniture, the sellers were contrary, the agents were uncooperative, and Michael felt tempted to behave just as badly, or in his words, "like a jerk."

Michael was stuck in Safety Consciousness. His first thought was to back out of the deal. Instead, he decided to enter Heart Consciousness. He thought about how grateful he was to get the house in a seller's market. The sellers had received a number of offers and could have chosen someone else. Shifting into Heart changed the picture in Michael's mind. He felt fortunate that he could afford to pay the extra money. And he didn't want to move into a new home feeling as if he'd been taken advantage of and being angry at the previous owners. From Heart Consciousness, he could walk into his new house and enjoy how spectacular it is. In Michael's case, entering Heart Consciousness changed his experience.

In Heart Consciousness, we may feel vulnerable, but we experience vulnerability as an opening. It deepens our connection with others. It is something to embrace. Some people think vulnerability is risky or scary because they are thinking about being vulnerable while they are in Safety Consciousness. It's different in Heart.

In Heart, depending on the task at hand, we can still be as productive as we are when in Safety–Reward, but we tend to go slower, multitask less, and do fewer things. Ironically, we may get more done, enjoy ourselves more, and form stronger connections with others.

We're not suggesting that Heart Consciousness is always appropriate or accessible. There are times when we need to stay in Safety Consciousness, focusing on a difficult task, setting boundaries to protect ourselves or loved ones, or expressing emotions such as anger or disappointment that arise in

Safety Consciousness. But when we're ready to move on, appreciating the life we have, our capabilities, friends, dreams, and the beauty that surrounds us, Heart Consciousness is waiting for us.

But even Heart Consciousness has its limits. If we want to move beyond the states of consciousness that involve thinking, internal dialogue, and evaluation, we can shift into Spacious Consciousness.

SPACIOUS CONSCIOUSNESS

In Spacious Consciousness, we transcend our typical experience of being in the world. Our perception of time is altered, and we experience timelessness—we abandon the angst and urgency associated with time. We aren't burdened by our past, and we aren't worried about our future. Instead of pressing to reach a conclusion and forcing things to happen, we experience a unique state of presence. No agenda, no effort, no measurements.

Spaciousness is a felt state more than a thinking state. There are few words. Time and words are replaced with space and awareness. Colors appear brighter and scents and sounds more distinctive as our sense of self becomes boundless. We feel that we are part of something much larger than ourselves, and we have no concerns.

When we practice the A.W.E. Method, we are intentionally accessing Spacious Consciousness because awe is a part of spaciousness. But spaciousness is bigger than awe.

Spaciousness has a range. At the far end we are in a state of pure presence, deeply relaxed in a predominantly parasympathetic state with no mental chatter. Other experiences of spaciousness, such as chanting, prayer, and awe, have some degree of sympathetic arousal.

Just as we don't live in awe all the time, we don't dwell in spaciousness; we visit spaciousness, opening ourselves to the abundance of beauty and innate wisdom that life—the universe—offers us. We then bring an expansive quality back into our daily lives. This expansiveness—ease, loosening, relaxing—allows us to change our lives in ways we could previously only imagine.

Facing a challenging situation, like losing a job, becomes one small event in the course of a life and an even smaller event in the course of all lives. It's as if we relax our grip on how things should be and open ourselves to possibilities. This is when profound growth and change can happen. How? Spaciousness disrupts our connection to our identity—how we perceive ourselves—so that we feel less attached to our story and can change it.

Does spaciousness solve all our problems? No, because we can't live in that state all the time. But each time we visit spaciousness, we reset our nervous system so that we are more resilient, curious, open, and less reactive and attached to old dysfunctional patterns that were born in Safety Consciousness. We may still feel a sense of peace regardless of what happens in our life. This is the cumulative physiological, psychological, and spiritual effect of awe.

One caveat about Spacious Consciousness is that it's tempting to want to go there often, sometimes to escape or deny our responsibilities—to do what's known as spiritual bypassing. Using Spacious Consciousness to bypass problems that require our attention doesn't work in the long run.

If we want to live in the world, hold a job, be in relationship, and deal well with our children, our aging parents, and our own process of aging, we must learn to fluidly move through all states of consciousness: Safety, Heart, and Spacious. Yet most of us spend a disproportionate amount of time in Safety.

Life's ups and downs can bring us back to Safety Consciousness when we'd rather be in Heart or Spacious. To stay in Heart and Spacious for longer periods of time, we need to master how to move between levels on command.

MASTERING THE 3LC—WITH A.W.E.

Deciding to intentionally change levels of consciousness requires some practice. It begins by asking yourself three questions: *What state of consciousness am I in? Is this where I want to be?* If the answer is no, ask yourself, *What state of consciousness do I want to be in?* Your answer will depend on the context.

When you're in Safety–Threat and the threat is severe—say, you're being chased by a grizzly—you're not going to be able to shift to any other level. The body's fight-flight-freeze mechanism is too powerful. The amygdala is at full throttle, taking advantage of every survival instinct you have. The rest of your brain is not going to ponder levels of consciousness. If you're in Safety–Threat because you're truly in danger, you probably need to be in Safety–Threat.

But if you can engage your neocortex enough to ask the first question, that suggests the level of threat is manageable, and you may be able to shift your state of consciousness. Asking the three questions gives you enough self-awareness to get some perspective, and that's the place from which you can make choices.

Erin was a participant in one of our studies who quickly adopted the 3LC model and used it to transform her relationship to her work.

Two nights a week I leave for work at 9:50 p.m. It takes me forty minutes to get to work. I work for an hour to an hour and a half and then make up my bed in the spare room of my client's home and go to sleep. It takes a long time to go to sleep. I don't like the bed. It's too soft for me, as my sixty-five-year-old body prefers more support. I average five hours of sleep. In the morning I spend the next two to three hours working and then I leave.

When I think about those nights of going to work downtown—walking the long blocks to and from the subway in the cold winter or on the hot and hectic summer nights—I dread going to work. I hate the idea. I am in full resistance mode. When I stop and ask myself what state of consciousness I'm in, I know I'm in Safety Consciousness, and I realize that makes no sense.

My job consists of helping one of my dearest friends into bed and then in the morning, helping him get up and ready for the day. My friend broke his neck nineteen years ago. He and I have been working together for thirteen years.

My friend has had help going to bed and getting up in the morning every day for nineteen years. In all these years, he's never showered alone. When I take a moment and imagine being in his body, I immediately shift to Heart

Consciousness. Then, even though it's late, cold, rainy, and dark when I leave my apartment, I am smiling and grateful for the walk to the subway. My goal every time I go to work is to be the person I would want to help me if our roles were reversed.[1]

There's no prescription or hard-and-fast rules for when to change your level of consciousness. It's really quite personal. Our rule of thumb? If you don't like how you're feeling—if you are uncomfortable, worried, or upset, and the tension is building—shift gears.

Accessing Heart Consciousness is natural and requires only that we focus on what we appreciate or are grateful for. Shifting into Spacious Consciousness, although also very natural, has traditionally been thought to require time, effort, and dedication to a mindfulness practice. The A.W.E. Method, however, is a shortcut into spaciousness and awe, quickly taking us to a perspective that dramatically alters the way we feel, see the world, relate to people, and interpret events.

By using the A.W.E. Method to find awe, we can move directly from Safety Consciousness, where energy is constrained and limited, into Spacious Consciousness, where energy is in abundance.

Spacious Consciousness helps us release stress and tension. In a more relaxed state, we have greater flexibility and can make conscious choices about whether to go back to Safety or Heart. Because we've shifted our energy, we are in a better place to make those decisions.

One of Jake's clients, Trevor, labeled himself an insomniac. After learning to use A.W.E., two things happened. First, Trevor stopped referring to himself as an insomniac. When Jake asked him why, he said, "I realize I'm lots of things. My insomnia is one small part of a much larger picture." This was a sign that Trevor's identity was expanding as a result of practicing A.W.E. The second thing that happened? He started sleeping well. He explained it this way:

I go outside at night just before I go to bed. I practice A.W.E. while I look up at the stars, imagining that the light I see has been traveling a long time before it reaches my eyes. For example, the light from the nearest star, which is Alpha Centauri, takes 4.22 light-years to reach us. So, although I'm seeing that star, it may not even exist anymore. I'm just seeing the light that was there over four years ago. This makes me wonder about everything I see and how real it is. Somehow, that makes me relax. I can't explain it, but it's as if I disconnect from my worries.[2]

Safety is a valuable and necessary state of consciousness. Paradoxically, mastering Safety ensures we can spend more time in Heart and Spacious. While the latter give us fresh perspectives, Safety is where we take responsibility for setting a solid foundation for our lives so that we feel generally empowered. It's where we solve problems by taking action and setting boundaries in our relationships.

Depending on both historical and current events, some people will find it more challenging than others to create a feeling of safety. People with a history of trauma and those who are required to go into spaces they experience as unsafe—school, work, home—have a greater challenge. In these and other situations, we need to choose the level of consciousness that is most helpful for us.

MEDITATION FOR SHIFTING YOUR LEVEL OF CONSCIOUSNESS

If accessing different levels of consciousness in your life feels difficult, we encourage you to start by accessing different levels of consciousness within the privacy of your mind. Jake offers this meditation to his clients as a tool they can use to access the 3LC. Because it involves closing your eyes, feel free to make a voice memo or otherwise record yourself reading the meditation so that you can play it back. To listen to a recording of the meditation, you can also visit our website at ThePowerOfAwe.com.

To begin, sit on a cushion or in a chair, in a comfortable position with your spine erect if possible. If it's comfortable, cross your ankles and allow your hands to rest in your lap with the tips of your index fingers touching the tips of your thumbs.

Breathe normally, relaxing more with each breath. As you continue breathing, close your eyes. Take a moment to imagine a small light in the center of your head. With each breath, allow the light to grow larger and stronger. As the light grows, it fills your head, expanding with each breath, extending beyond your head, growing in every direction. Imagine the light expands in front of you, behind you, to both sides, as well as above and below you. This light represents an energy field that can extend several feet beyond your body in every direction.

Allow yourself to be aware of this energy field, this large sphere of light that surrounds you. This is a place to be present and rest for a few minutes. You can say in your own mind, "I disinvite any thoughts or intrusions from being in this space for the next few minutes."

As you continue breathing, place your attention at the base of your spine. Notice the quality of the energy at the base of your spine. Imagine this is the home of Safety Consciousness, an extremely valuable state of consciousness that is with us from the time we are born until the time we die.

As you focus on Safety Consciousness, if you're comfortable doing so, begin breathing in the nose and out the mouth. As you're doing so, I'm going to express some of the things you may feel when in Safety Consciousness. Just continue breathing in the nose, out the mouth, and notice any sensations in your body. Okay, here we go:

Sometimes I feel driven to do things.

Sometimes I feel at a loss.

Sometimes I feel smart.

Sometimes I feel like I don't know what to do.

Sometimes I feel determined.

Sometimes I feel like I need help.

Sometimes I feel like helping others.

Continue breathing in the nose, out the mouth.

All these feelings arise within Safety Consciousness. Each one of these feelings is possible because you are alive. Safety Consciousness is a state of being in which we experience our needs and vulnerabilities, and we make plans, take actions, and set boundaries to help us navigate life. Safety Consciousness spurs us to find solutions that help us grow and feel more secure.

Take a moment to appreciate Safety Consciousness, trusting your instincts, skills, and insights to guide you—providing a strong foundation upon which to build your life. Much that you have and value is the result of managing your life in Safety Consciousness.

As you take a few moments to appreciate all that Safety Consciousness offers you, you may begin to feel the energy at the base of your spine start to rise. Just notice. The act of appreciation can help shift our state of being. If you feel the energy rising, allow it to continue. If not, imagine the energy rising. Encourage the energy in the base of your spine to flow up into your heart center.

Continue breathing, but breathe in the nose, out the nose—if that's comfortable for you. As you access Heart Consciousness, take a few moments to appreciate the people in your life who you love and the people who love you. Appreciate the pets you may have in your life and the places you love to visit. Appreciate the gifts you have and the qualities you value about yourself. Appreciate the beauty. Rest in the beauty.

Pause for a few moments. Notice the sensations in your body and the quality of being in Heart Consciousness.

You may begin to notice the energy in your spine starting to rise again. If so, allow it to rise. Or imagine it flowing up your spine, into your head. The energy may even continue to rise through and beyond your head.

As the energy rises, you may become aware of Spacious Consciousness, a state in which there are no words. This is a state of expanding awareness and timelessness. There is no need to track or describe, just be in this expansive state for a few moments. Breathing, relaxing, expanding. Boundless. Spacious presence.

Notice the overall sensation of being in this state. Notice if it is familiar or unfamiliar. Experience this way of being that is effortless.

Pause.

When you feel ready to bring this meditation to a close, allow the energy to drift back down from your head to your heart. Pause for a moment to reexperience Heart Consciousness—a state of deep appreciation. Be aware of any changes in your body as you do this.

And then when you are ready, allow the energy to drift back down from your heart to the bottom of your spine—to Safety Consciousness—the foundation upon which you live your life. Pause for a moment and notice any sensations in your body.

When you are ready, open your eyes.

The more you practice moving from one state of consciousness to another, the easier it becomes. We often rest in Safety Consciousness out of habit, and yet we can shift our state of consciousness by shifting our attention.

In the next section, we show you what it means to live life without the glass ceiling formed by fear and anxiety—even during the worst of times.

PART IV

A.W.E. WHEREVER YOU ARE

CHAPTER 10

FINDING AWE IN TIMES OF STRIFE

A.W.E. asks us to focus on something we value, appreciate, or find amazing. But how do we find awe when riots, crime, pandemics, climate change, social injustice, and political and economic strife and uncertainty surround us? How do we muster the motivation to practice A.W.E. while going through a divorce, after getting a cancer diagnosis, or when we've just lost a loved one?

The power of a painful emotion can pull our attention away from that which nourishes our souls—from what is most precious to us. But the things in life that are awesome, beautiful, surreal, and profound still exist around us and in us even when life is difficult. Awe is a special emotion in that it can reconnect us with what is most precious, even during the worst of times.

THE UNIQUE ABILITY OF AWE

Viktor Frankl, Holocaust survivor and author of *Man's Search for Meaning*, describes a moment of awe while he was a prisoner in a Nazi concentration camp during World War II:

If someone had seen our faces on the journey from Auschwitz to a Bavarian camp as we beheld the mountains of Salzburg with their summits glowing in the sunset, through the little barred windows of the prison carriage, he would never have believed that those were the faces of men who had given up all hope of life and liberty.[1]

Awe can bring us back to what is precious, in part because it has the unique ability to be present with other emotions, including—as Frankl and his prison mates experienced—hopelessness. When we're unhappy, for example, we may not be able to access happiness at the same time. And when we're anxious, we may not be able to relax at the same time. But whether we feel unhappy or happy, anxious or relaxed, we can also feel awe. That we have the capacity to be in awe when experiencing difficult emotions gives us a great deal of influence over our suffering.

During painful and difficult times, it's all too easy to fixate on the cause of our pain as if it were the bull's-eye of a target. This might be useful as we try to make sense of what's happening and maybe even solve the problem. But energy follows attention, so what we focus on can grow in magnitude, so much so that the loss or concern can overshadow what is good in our world, at least in our minds. It's easy to lose sight of the bigger picture, the outer rings of the target, including perhaps the people who love us, the people we love, and that our life has meaning, purpose, and potential. Those outer rings are important because they encompass the things we value, appreciate, or find amazing. With them, we experience life from a more holistic perspective.

Winston Churchill once said, "If you're going through hell, keep going." Awe helps us do just that. Awe is a vehicle that takes us to the other side of the pain and back to what is precious.

AN A.W.E. MOMENT

You can train yourself to focus less on the bull's-eye (the cause of your suffering) and more on the outer rings (big picture) by doing this Elevate Your Gaze exercise in peripheral vision:

Take a walk in the woods or a park. Choose a quiet setting with a path that's fairly level and clear of any obstacles. Begin walking slowly, grounding yourself with each step that you take. Now elevate your eyes so that your view is straight out in front of you rather than lowered toward the ground. If thoughts arise, you'll likely find your gaze has gravitated toward the ground. If this happens, just notice and elevate your eyes again.

Now, while continuing to walk, take a deep breath, relax, and without moving your eyes to the side, expand your peripheral field of vision, taking in all you can see to either side of you. You'll begin to see you have a larger window on the world, not just the focused area in front of you. Once this happens, you may begin to perceive the world as moving past you, instead of you moving yourself through the world.

Please note: When doing this, look at the path ahead to assess the terrain as often as you need to.

FINDING THE COLLATERAL BEAUTY

Sadness, fear, anxiety, loneliness, and loss are born out of something precious. The gut-wrenching loneliness that comes with losing a loved one, for instance, is rooted in love. Healing from the pain of loss is hard for most of us because, to heal, we're required to go *through* the pain. But we tend to resist this dark side of the experience—the prospect of being alone and lonely, for instance—because when we connect with this dark side, something happens: We disconnect from what is precious to us—in this case, love. This disconnection amplifies the pain. But when we finally go beyond this sadness and loneliness, we can reconnect with what is precious to us and ease the pain. So there's a collateral beauty to emotional pain. It guides us back to what is precious.

For example, after losing a dog that's been our companion for fifteen years, we focus first on the emptiness and quiet in the house, the basket of unused toys, and the lonely leash hanging in the utility room. Looking at old photos of our dog, our eyes tear up as we recall the companionship our pet gave us on hikes and how gentle he was with the kids. We connect with our sadness.

But we can also remember and reexperience the joy, tenderness, and comfort of having had a relationship with our pet—the collateral beauty. That's what is called a holistic experience. There is something extremely grounding about feeling the totality of the experience—the pain and the love. We're left feeling the fullness of life.

In *The Order of Time*, physicist and author Carlo Rovelli sums up this dynamic beautifully: "It isn't absence that causes sorrow. It is affection and love. Without affection, without love, such absences would cause us no pain. For this reason, even the pain caused by absence is, in the end, something good and even beautiful, because it feeds on that which gives meaning to life."[2]

Getting to that point is, for many people, a long and arduous process. All emotions are temporary, but moving through negative emotions can be cyclical. One day we feel the collateral beauty and the next week it's gone. We may have good days, weeks, months, or years and then fall back into our grief. Time, accompanied by support and acceptance, is the traditional path to healing. But we now understand that awe is another option. Awe helps us navigate difficult emotions by creating a different focus for our attention and shifting our level of consciousness.

In awe, instead of getting lost in the small picture of the pain, we connect with the bigger picture, which includes the profound, the timeless, the beauty. It's the sunset the prisoner sees cased in the mountains of Salzburg. Awe doesn't take away our pain. Awe spurs the cognitive accommodation that offers a new perspective so that we can appreciate the entirety of what we're feeling, whatever that might be.

The A.W.E. Method, then, can help to end the cyclical nature of some painful experiences by quickly and repeatedly bringing us back to what is precious. We can use A.W.E. to experience the collateral beauty at will.

In an essay, clinical psychologist David Elkins (who, by the way, studied under Frankl) highlights the transformative element of awe. He describes moments of awe as "the most important, transformative experiences of life. . . . Awe is a lightning bolt that marks in memory those moments when the doors of perception are cleansed and we see with startling clarity what is truly important in life."[3]

The A.W.E. practice is useful in helping us connect to awe and reconnect to what is precious and truly important, even for five or fifteen seconds. Feeling the confusingly incredible awe of being alive disorients us so that we don't feel the immediacy of our suffering but rather the vastness of our life. The bull's-eye is no more, at least for the moment. Though we will likely return to our sadness or suffering, we can also return to awe. As a conduit to returning to what is precious, A.W.E., then, helps us to heal.

A.W.E. won't solve all our problems, much less the world's problems, in five seconds. A.W.E. is less a technique to solve problems than a practice that takes us to a different state of consciousness—Spacious Consciousness—which means we're less likely to have thoughts and beliefs that keep us stuck in Safety Consciousness when it's not helpful. Visiting awe frequently is, in a sense, a preventive measure because awe can establish new neural pathways that reconnect us to what is precious to us. We talk about this more in Chapter 11.

Awe is helpful during good and bad times. But it can feel especially relevant during times of strife. Physiologically, it creates coherence, quiets the default mode network, and increases ventral vagal tone, all of which contribute to calming the nervous system so that we feel safe enough to heal.

Yet when we're in the thick of emotional distress, finding awe is not typically front and center. Five patterns may surface when people go through a hard time. Most of us are familiar with one or all of these patterns, even if we've never articulated them. Understanding these dynamics intellectually won't necessarily be enough to help reconnect to what is precious. But recognizing them may be a cue to practice A.W.E.

> Life can be a challenge and having tools to remind myself of who and where I am in that world and what is most important is priceless. . . . A.W.E. is a simple tool that takes me away from the chaos of our world and reminds me that the experience of being alive is the true value.[4]
>
> —Tom

FIVE PATTERNS OF STRIFE

Emotional suffering may cause us to lose perspective and get tangled in any of five dynamics: attaching, resisting, victimizing, catastrophizing, and withdrawing. Each of these five patterns has an opposite—a state of mind that feels out of reach, even unfathomable, when we've discomforted ourselves so much that we can't see a way out of our worry or grief. But a growing body of research supports that, regardless of which pattern strife manifests through, awe is helpful in disrupting it. It provides the cognitive accommodation awe researchers talk about.

Awe can awaken us and move us through our thought patterns to fresh and often opposite perspectives. It's possible, for example, to go from scarcity to abundance, aversion to acceptance, disempowerment to empowerment, and disconnection to connection. And awe helps us rewrite the stories we're telling ourselves, the stories that are often rooted in anxiety and Safety Consciousness that can keep us stuck.

Some of us tend to fall into specific repetitive patterns that then become our modus operandi. Even if the patterns may be uncomfortable, they are at least familiar. A regular A.W.E. practice can dislodge these patterns so that when times of strife occur, we are better able to handle the waves of emotions. Or we might spontaneously move into awe, where we can see the bigger picture, write a better story, choose empowerment, and lean into our relationships instead of withdrawing. It's refreshing to think that anxiety, anguish, and disempowerment can be eased. Done in the right circumstances, this process is transformative.

Also, if we recognize these patterns in others, we can be more helpful—possibly pointing out the pattern, or at least not commiserating with them. And we may have more understanding and compassion because we're better able to hold a big-picture view.

Following are descriptions of each of the patterns. See if any of them sound familiar.

ATTACHMENT

Attachment is holding onto something, most often an ideal, to the point where we become rigid about how things are supposed to be. When a gap opens between our expectations and our reality—when life doesn't go according to our ideal—attachment to our ideal can cause us to feel dissatisfied and tension builds.

Attachment has a clinging quality to it that's well illustrated with Judy's story. Judy, who was in our pilot project, talked often about her eighteen-year-old son, Kyle. A great athlete and highly personable, Kyle had recently dropped out of college. Judy was beside herself. She was convinced that Kyle would make the perfect sports medicine physician, but Kyle had a different plan. He took a minimum-wage, low-stress job. Judy was so attached to her plans for Kyle that when he didn't follow through with them, she suffered. And her suffering caused a great deal of tension in their relationship and beyond. It affected the entirety of her life. In her words, she was "despairing, depressed, and joyless" for at least six months.

The solution to attaching is to do the opposite: In this case, let go, which usually requires some humility as well as taking other perspectives into consideration. In Judy's case, that meant being able to see her son for who he was instead who she wanted him to be. Releasing our attachment puts us back in the flow, going with what is and being present.

Getting to the point where we're ready to let go can be a process. But awe can help by disrupting the intense attachment that we have, along with the beliefs that we've adopted without even knowing we've adopted them. Awe creates a sense that there is more to life than our self-interests, and this new perspective is broader, going well beyond just a "me" perspective.

Awe mitigates fears about letting go and breaking free of a scarcity mentality. In awe, we are able to more easily let go and adapt to our new set of circumstances because the cognitive accommodation offers us a different perspective, a new way of seeing the situation. At this point we don't mind because awe takes us to a place greater than what we're attached to. It opens us to a world of unlimited possibilities.

Using A.W.E.—experiencing this disruption on and off throughout the day and in the ordinary—has a pervasive effect. We're more relaxed in general, and we're not grasping so tightly.

RESISTING

Resisting and attachment are two sides of the same coin. Most of us know the feeling of being attached to what we want while simultaneously resisting what we don't want. We can be attached to our youthfulness and resist aging, for instance. Resisting, however, has a different energic quality than attachment. Resisting involves pushing away what we don't want by repressing it, denying it, or distracting ourselves. It's common to resist things we perceive as negative. It's also really tiring. Denying our perception of reality takes a good amount of energy.

To recognize when we are resisting, it can help to look at recurring patterns in our life. If we repeatedly attract the wrong partner or sabotage our success, it might be a sign that we are resisting some "truth." If we keep doing the same thing over and over again while expecting different results—we're demonstrating the casual definition of insanity.

To distance ourselves from what we don't want to experience, we might distract ourselves—in positive or negative ways—by immersing ourselves in a hobby or creative project, for instance, or alternatively, overworking or drinking too much. Not wanting to deal with a bad marriage, for example, we might resist having "the hard conversation." Resisting may save us from feeling negative emotions, but it also disconnects us from the positive—from what is precious to us.

We might choose to resist any number of things. Aging is a big one for many people because they perceive most of what goes with it as negative—failing bodies, fading beauty, diminished sense of power over their autonomy. They might refuse care, resist giving up the keys to their car, insist on climbing up a wobbly ladder to clean the gutters. Awe helps with resistance by putting us in a different frame of mind: acceptance.

Phyllis, age ninety-two, was married to one of the world's leading dolphin experts. With her husband, son, and three daughters, she traveled the world and spent most of her time living on its beautiful oceans. She led a full, if not enviable, life.

As Phyllis has aged, she has lost the ability to walk and now uses a wheelchair. Losing this ability can be traumatic. For Phyllis, it became a source of curiosity. "I've never experienced being in a wheelchair before," she told Michael, who has known her for thirty years:

I could mourn the loss of my legs, but I have a choice in how to respond to what is happening to me. Riding in a wheelchair is an amazing life experience. I'm just fascinated by this new experience of being wheeled around and so grateful I'm alive, with my family's support and the abundance of wonder in my life.

The world is overflowing with love. The world is full of excitement. The world is full of curiosity and awe. Life is wonderful. There is so much happening to me that is so much fun.

I know I'm aging. [But] I'm super curious and in awe about everything in my life. Today I was in awe of playing with the dogs. I look outside my window and there are wonderful things happening all the time. I get to see the birds, the squirrels, the trees, and the clouds in the sky. I'm just fascinated by the natural world. I just learned that the wishbones on the chests of the wild turkeys that walk through my yard date back to the time of the dinosaurs. That is amazing! I wake every day in anticipation for all the beautiful and exciting things I get to experience. Why resist when there is so much to embrace every day!

In response to the COVID-19 pandemic and other disconcerting news of the world, Phyllis said, with complete acceptance, that "there is no normal. The only constant is that change happens every day. Every day is very exciting. Keep smiling. I'm so lucky that I have my family, three daughters just a stone's throw away."[5]

Another monumental example of acceptance comes from John Weir, the codeveloper of Perception Language. While conducting one of his last personal development workshops, John approached aging in a manner similar to Phyllis. During an experiential exercise one day, he became intrigued when he realized he could no longer roll over onto his belly from his back. He marveled at how, at age eighty-five, he had returned to being as helpless as a two-month-old. Rather than deny or get sad or angry over his loss of function, he was curious about what it means to live in a human body. In awe, he was fascinated by this new sensation, this new discovery about his body.

Phyllis and John are exceptions in terms of how they have handled the challenges that come with aging. Yet, we can learn from them as examples of people who use A.W.E. When in awe, we stop labeling things as negative and have a greater degree of acceptance. In one study, people who were induced to feel awe "present[ed] a more balanced view of their strengths and weaknesses to others and acknowledge[d], to a greater degree, the contribution of outside forces in their own personal accomplishments."[6] Awe encourages humility, and when humble, we're more accepting and less judgmental. We can see things without being so reactive. Awe gives us a break from processing and judging unwanted events and gives us the capacity to see through them—to see a larger picture, the outer rings of the target. We can then approach the event with curiosity and openness.

CATASTROPHIZING

Catastrophizing is blowing things out of proportion. Mostly we're just thinking about what could go wrong—*What if I fail? What if my plan doesn't work? What if the economy collapses?* This internal dialogue of worst-case-scenario projections creates a convincing story that causes us to lose hope about the future, which can lead to depression, despair, or anger.

Some of us catastrophize more than others, but even the most even-keeled are prone to it in some circumstances. When Bob, one of Jake's clients and a highly competent business executive, learned some disturbing information about his company, he was so confident and capable and could rely on such good resources that he and his team passed catastrophizing and went directly into problem-solving mode. But when it came to his health, Bob was less confident. When his doctor gave him a serious medical diagnosis, his first thoughts were worst-case scenarios. All he could think of was that his father had had a similar diagnosis that resulted in premature death.

Cynthia, another of Jake's clients, fell prey to catastrophizing during the pandemic, which also corresponded with social unrest and political and economic uncertainty. *If I get COVID-19, will I be able to get a hospital bed? Will I die? Will I infect my family? Am I going to lose my business? Will I ever be able to return to work? Chaos is erupting all around us. The world will never be the same.* Cynthia wasn't alone. During the height of the pandemic, many people lived in Safety Consciousness.

Awe can't abort a pandemic or change a medical diagnosis or economic uncertainty, but awe addresses catastrophizing in several ways. In a study about the discomfort some of us feel while waiting for a test result or a diagnosis, for instance, researchers learned that awe decreased anxiety and improved well-being and positive emotions.[7] Awe puts us in Spacious Consciousness and so takes away that piece that has to do with time—in this case, the future. And because awe is a nonverbal state, we stop telling ourselves threatening narratives. When we return to Safety Consciousness, our stories have changed so that our internal dialogue is lighter.

When catastrophizing, some of us make the problem all about us. When that happens, we fall into victimizing.

VICTIMIZING

Victimizing often contains the thought *Why me?* or *It's not fair.* And it can have a self-indulgent quality to it: We take another person's difficulty and make it about ourselves. For example, the husband who talks about his wife's illness, not in terms of how much she's suffering but in terms of what a burden it is on him to take care of her, is victimizing himself.

There are circumstances in which people are subjected to violence and are victims, or survivors, and it's not inappropriate that they identify as victims. Hopefully, that's a temporary identity. Victimizing, as we're using it here, refers to the everyday situations in which people make themselves feel like victims because they perceive someone or something has wronged them.

We've all felt the victim and that sense of hurt, disbelief, and indignation. The offense is usually bad enough, but we make it worse when we think of ourselves as victims. We victimize ourselves when we believe that we have been wronged—and then act as if the one who harmed us is responsible for how we feel about what happened.

Buddhists talk about victimization in a parable of two arrows. The first arrow—a misfortunate event that befalls us—is painful, but we can't always control whether we're in the line of fire. The second arrow is our reaction to the first arrow—and when it's victimizing, it causes more suffering. However, this second arrow is optional.

By definition, victims feel powerless. When we see ourselves as a victim, we disempower ourselves and are unable to act on our own behalf. Instead, we expect someone else—the person who harmed us—to ease our suffering. Put this way, giving so much power to the perpetrator (a person, organization, society, government—you name it) can be ludicrous. Yet we do it often when we blame others for how we feel.

It may sound harsh, but victimizing is one way to skirt taking responsibility for our emotions and sometimes our actions. Most of the time we don't realize we're doing it. Unless we become more conscious of victimizing, it's hard to see, especially because it's so pervasive in our society.

This is a story that illustrates how one woman used the Three Levels of Consciousness and A.W.E. to sidestep victimizing.

Jade was a practitioner of the Three Levels of Consciousness model and well versed in A.W.E. before she was literally run over by a truck while walking across the street one hot summer day. While lying on the ground in severe pain, Jade was remarkably composed. Her first thought was *I have a choice in how I respond to this life-altering event that just happened to me.* She then thought about the welfare of the person who was crossing the street with her. *Was he hurt too?* And then she started thinking about how she would need to manage herself to get through what she knew was a life-changing experience.

Surrounded by the chaos of first responders and onlookers, Jade became very present. She acknowledged the agonizing pain in her right leg but knew to broaden her attention, which she did by inhaling the smell of the pavement and feeling the sun's warmth. She took deep breaths in through her nose and exhaled slowly and completely out of her mouth. She told herself she was okay in this moment. And she spoke sweetly and calmly to her body and nervous system.

During a monthlong hospital stay, Jade made sure to tend to her needs. If she was tired, she rested. If she needed help, she asked for it. But for much of her stay, she chose to help others. Instead of being angry or bitter at the truck driver, she focused on the people who were trying to help her—looking into the eyes of hospital staff and expressing her gratitude for their attention. In a wheelchair, Jade visited other patients on her floor and talked to them about their families and the reason for their hospital stay. She even brought her less mobile roommate treats and warm washcloths with which to wash her face and hands. By helping others, Jade was actually enjoying her time in the hospital, despite facing the prospect of not being able to walk again.

Jade, refusing to victimize herself, eventually recovered some of her ability, but she continues to have limitations compared to before the accident, when she led an active life.

Awe is not typically useful in highly traumatic situations such as the one Jade experienced. As we discussed earlier, when under severe threat, the brain is hijacked by the amygdala, and we go into a fight-flight-freeze response.

However, Jade's story illustrates that an experienced practitioner can use awe to temper the autonomic nervous system response even in highly charged situations.

Awe can help us avoid victimizing and instead feel empowered, not by making us feel bigger but, paradoxically, by making us feel smaller. When researchers from the Netherlands showed three groups of participants slides of spectacular, mundane, or neutral scenes in nature, those in the group that witnessed the spectacular described not only feeling awe but also what awe researchers have termed "the small self" or "the diminished self." In relation to their surroundings—these extraordinary pictures of nature—they felt insignificant.[8] Awe effectively shifts our focus from the bull's-eye to the outer rings of the target. No longer as focused on our self, our concerns are less relevant, so we are less likely to be self-indulgent.

WITHDRAWING

When going through times of strife, some people turn away from others. There is a wide variety of reasons why people do this. Some don't want to be seen as needy or vulnerable. Others might need time to process their feelings and events. So, although withdrawal serves its purpose in the short term, holding on to this pattern past its expiration date leads to disconnection and loneliness. Not returning phone calls or being only half present during a conversation, for instance, sends the message that we don't want to talk to our support system, and eventually these trusted allies of ours stop reaching out.

Withdrawing leads to isolation, which leads to loneliness, which we talked about in Chapter 1. We humans are wired to connect. Withdrawing, especially when we need support, exacerbates emotional suffering. Feeling connected and getting emotional support from others helps us lift ourselves out of our pain.

When it comes to loneliness, awe does two things: First, it helps us connect to something greater than ourselves—a higher power, spiritual tradition, nature, being of service. Second, awe calms the nervous system and promotes prosocial behaviors, making us more available to connect with others. One of the most amazing aspects of awe is that we can generate feelings of connection independent of other people. We can be alone in a remote hut on the Arctic Circle and feel a sense of connection that minimizes loneliness.

Don, a participant in one of our studies, used awe to engage in life even when literally isolated. Diagnosed with blood cancer, Don spent up to four weeks at a time in isolation at the hospital undergoing bone marrow transplants and other treatments. Instead of withdrawing, he dove into the A.W.E. practice and spent much of his day in awe. He covered a wall in his room with photos of people and things that inspired awe in him—his family, his pets, places he loved to visit. He used those images and memories to transport himself into a state of awe, feeling what he called a "vast connection." And he looked for moments of awe while interacting with his doctors and nurses—appreciating their care and commitment. In pain and solitude, Don cultivated enormous gratitude by using A.W.E.

AN A.W.E. MOMENT

When stuck in one of the five patterns of strife, we are also in a particular state of consciousness—Safety. If we are truly feeling unsafe, we might want to start by using Perception Language, which creates a greater sense of safety because we empower ourselves. When we feel safer, awe is more accessible.

When Perception Language is combined with A.W.E., the two work together to fuel transformation. We invite you to try it. The next time you go through a hard time, use Perception Language to realize and remember that whatever feelings you have—whether you're attaching, resisting, victimizing, catastrophizing, or withdrawing—you're doing these things to yourself based on how you're making meaning of the situation.

(continues)

(continued)

If you're doing these things to yourself, then you have the power to do something different. Recognizing you have choice, you feel safer. Once you feel safer, you can use the A.W.E. Method to place your attention on something other than the bull's-eye. You can expand your perspective.

RIDING THE WAVES

Cheryl, one of Michael's long-term patients, provides an example of how multiple patterns of strife can interact. Cheryl suffered from chronic neck and low back pain after an injury and had previously undergone cervical spine surgery for herniated disks in her neck. The surgery helped relieve some of the pain radiating down her arms but caused scar tissue to develop in her neck, and she subsequently developed chronic cervicogenic head-aches. She occasionally required emergency room visits for injections of pain medication to abort her headaches.

When she participated in Michael's A.W.E. class, Cheryl was about to become a grandmother for the first time, and she was terribly concerned that she wouldn't be able to hold her grandchild in her arms without worsening her pain. By the second group session, she said she was able to stop her head-aches without an emergency room visit for the first time. Six months later, Cheryl told Michael that the A.W.E Method gave her near total control over her headaches and muscle tension, and that she felt happy once again. "Best of all," Cheryl said, "I can hold my grandchild."[9]

Before taking Michael's class, Cheryl was **attached** to the way things were. She held on to her ideas about how she was before her surgery. And she **resisted** the idea of having physical limitations and the need to modify her routines and lifestyle. At one point in the process, she was **catastrophizing**, *What if this gets worse, what if I can never hold my grandchild?* That led to some self-**victimization**: *Why me? It's not fair.* And the downward emotional process—in addition to the physical pain—caused her to **withdraw** from other people, which only increased her frustration and despair.

We have demonstrated that awe is a form of therapy that helps us shift out of any one of these dysfunctional patterns. Kirk Schneider, psychologist and author of *Awakening to Awe*, also considers awe to be a form of therapy. In a paper, he writes, "Formally, I define awe as the co-mingling of humility, reverence, and wonder before creation; informally, I understand it as the thrill . . . of living. Awe is not spotlighted very often as a therapeutic 'condition,' but in my work and that of many of my colleagues it is the sine qua non of healing."[10]

Awe is healing. It can improve relationships, solve problems, and reduce anxiety by giving us a new, lighter, more promising perspective.

While A.W.E. can help us through any of these five patterns, sometimes we can't quite put our finger on what's troubling us. This experience usually involves baffling and sometimes elusive existential anxiety.

A REMEDY FOR EXISTENTIAL ANXIETY

Unlike other forms of anxiety that might arise when under pressure to perform well, such as when taking a test or confronting a formidable obstacle, existential anxiety is different. First, it's not actionable—there's not much we can do to rid ourselves of this type of angst. Second, it's comparatively invisible. Although existential anxiety is omnipresent, many of us aren't aware of it. But we all experience it to some degree. We may not know it's there until something happens to stir it up and bring it to the forefront—a close encounter with death, a loss, a pandemic, a disaster—yet it's a universal experience.

Existential anxiety is not actionable because its causes are not resolvable:

- Knowing that we and all the people we love will die someday
- Uncertainty about the future
- Not being fully present

There's not a solution to mortality or uncertainty. And although we can make efforts to be more present, those are usually short-lived. Existential anxiety is almost impossible to escape because it is part of human existence. But that doesn't stop us from trying.

Mental health professionals, including Jake, have tried for years to come up with effective strategies for dealing with existential anxiety. Until recently, the only known remedies were religion, medication, denial, and distraction.

That people turn to religion to deal with existential anxiety is not new. Religion has for millennia been a source of comfort for the masses. Attributing events not under our control to the work of God and finding connection with a like-minded community through a place of worship and religious or spiritual events are comforting. As is agreeing to live by a set of virtues with the promise of eternal life as a reward. All this has a way of easing existential anxiety by giving us something reassuring to hold onto. In *Awakening to Awe*, Kirk Schneider talks about how religion can enliven us: "Awe, inspired through participation in the sacred practices of one's religious or spiritual belief system, fans the flame of spirit, that vital, mysterious animating force within each of us that unites mind, body, and soul."[11]

Antianxiety pills, antidepressants, benzodiazepines, and more recently psychedelics such as mushrooms and MDMA have been used to reduce symptoms of all types of anxiety, including existential. Medications are necessary, appropriate, and helpful in certain circumstances. In some cases, they are not always a true solution but a kind of medical bypassing, which is akin to the spiritual bypassing people sometimes use to avoid taking responsibility for problems in life.

Although many people actively pursue comfort in the face of existential anxiety through medication or religion, a great number of us deny its existence altogether. The recent COVID-19 pandemic became a proving ground for understanding what people will do in response to existential anxiety. Researchers learned that pandemics "activate mortality awareness" and that people basically respond in one (or more) of three ways: They become proactive and take measures to improve health and reduce their risk of exposure;

use maladaptive behaviors, which might include drinking too much or immersing themselves in social media, to keep the anxiety at bay; or deny the feelings of anxiety so they can distance themselves from the threat, in other words, believe the pandemic will not affect them personally.[12]

We have found that awe—remarkably—works to alleviate existential anxiety because it brings us out of Safety Consciousness (where existential anxiety arises) into Spacious Consciousness. When we access Spacious Consciousness, time, words, measurements, and comparisons don't exist, and so existential anxiety is no longer relevant.

Awe is a partial remedy in that it brings us to the present—and one of the reasons we aren't present is that we are distracting ourselves because of existential anxiety. Awe disrupts the distraction. When we access awe, we experience less anxiety in our lives overall. Feeling less anxious, we have less need to distract ourselves. It becomes a positive feedback loop.

For example, by accessing the awe that is connected to whatever we fear losing—such as a person we love—we connect with something greater than our anxiety. In part, this approach is a matter of switching focus from one side of a coin (fear of losing someone we love) to the other side of the same coin (the depth of our love for this person). It seems counterintuitive because we might think that if we feel our love more strongly, we would also feel more anxiety about losing the source of that love. But that's not what happens when we go fully into awe.

AN A.W.E. MOMENT

Think of a person you fear losing. Take a minute to get in touch with how much they mean to you. Give your full and undivided attention to how precious this person is to you. Be with those feelings and thoughts. Let them fill you. Then wait for the length of time

(continues)

(continued)

it takes for one inhalation, staying with the feelings and thoughts. When you exhale, allow your exhalation to be a little longer than normal and notice your positive feelings expand.

As we access awe, our concerns about time and loss are replaced with present-moment sensations that disrupt our anxious thoughts. The loss we fear is enveloped by our love and appreciation for that which we fear losing—whether person, place, thing, or idea.

Iva, a teacher and mother in her midthirties, used A.W.E. to deal with uncomfortable existential anxiety about her son:

> I scare myself often with the idea of my son dying. He's a very healthy five-year-old, and this fear is not based on any evidence. Furthermore, there is nothing in this anxiety that I can control. So, I stayed present with the fact that I get to be his mother. And I felt such awe when I realized how incredibly my life has changed because I get to be a mother. What an AWEsome gift! My heart, my face, my soul smile, and I feel ripples through my body. It's a long-lasting awe moment.[13]

Finding our way to the other side of anxiety connects us with our love and appreciation for being alive. The key is to move through the anxiety—not deny it—and when we do this, our relationship to anxiety shifts. Awe is a vehicle that takes us beyond the pain. It can ease our anxiety so that we can love more fully.

We're reminded of a quote from the movie *Shadowlands* in which author C. S. Lewis, played by Anthony Hopkins, describes what it is like to lose the love of his life: "Twice in that life I've been given the choice: as a boy and as a man. The boy chose safety, the man chooses suffering. The pain now is part of the happiness then. That's the deal."

If we are to love—life, a pet, a person, an accomplishment—we will experience loss. Worrying about that loss consciously or unconsciously creates anxiety. The anxiety inhibits our well-being and our relationships. Using the A.W.E. Method to experience awe turns down the volume of existential anxiety by helping us fully inhabit our love of life.

AWE OF GOD

When religious people experience awe of God, life improves markedly. In a unique study that assessed people's awe of God and compared it against life satisfaction, researchers from the University of Michigan found that church attendance led to greater practical wisdom via the lessons taught. In turn, people with practical wisdom tend to be more accepting of uncertainty and, in the study, were more open to experiencing awe of God. Likewise, these individuals felt more connected to others and were therefore more satisfied with life.

Although the researchers focused on awe of God, they acknowledged the impossibility of distinguishing between awe of God and the awe experienced outside of a religious context.[14] In other words, awe is awe, no matter how we access it.

Joyce, an elderly woman Jake worked with during the final months of her life, was small in stature—about a hundred pounds and a little over five feet tall—but she was large in spirit. She had led a remarkably joyful life, always active and adventuresome, so the limitations of infirmity raised her ire. This is why she contacted Jake; she didn't want to die angry. Jake describes how Joyce used A.W.E. to reengage the awe she felt in her youth:

Our time together was relatively brief, the last three months of her life. She quickly adopted the A.W.E. practice, in part, because she didn't know what else to do. And it was easy for her. She had lovely mementos throughout her home and ample natural beauty she could observe outside her window. But Joyce's strongest moments of awe were found in her memories.

One day I asked Joyce to think about a time when she felt strong and agile in her body. She closed her eyes and said, "I'm thinking about when I was an acrobatic horse rider, and I could stand in the saddle of a galloping horse." I encouraged her to give her full attention to that moment, standing in the saddle of the galloping horse. Even though she was lying in bed, I could see her posture shift, her spine arch, and her body expand as I gently guided her through the A.W.E. process.

After fifteen seconds I said, "Let your next out breath be a full exhale, deeper than normal." I witnessed her embody the experience. It was no longer a memory; it was a present moment of awe that offered a respite from her pain and sense of helplessness.

I asked Joyce to practice awe three times a day. She called me a couple of days later to thank me, saying, "I'd forgotten how beautiful my life has been and how much I love life."

When I visited her a week later, she said, "I've been a naughty gal," with a mischievous smile on her face.

"How naughty?"

She smiled again and said, "I practice A.W.E. all the time. Why would someone only want to do this three times a day?"

I spoke with Joyce two days before she passed away. Her daughter held the phone up so Joyce could hear me and say her final good-bye. All she said was "Awwwwwww."

Strife and painful events are part of life. Our reactions—including anxiety and hurt or sorrow—to unwelcome situations can pull us away from what is precious. Awe can take us through our discomfort by cleansing and broadening our perceptions—shifting our state of consciousness. It can also help us recognize unhealthy patterns we use when reacting to strife. Although awe can't always change our circumstances, a regular A.W.E. practice can help us navigate life's "downs" so that we remember what is precious.

CHAPTER 11

TWENTY-ONE DAYS OF A.W.E.

The world is full of magic things, patiently waiting for our senses to grow sharper.

—*William Butler Yeats*

The tree that moves some to tears of joy is to others a green thing that stands in the way.

—*William Blake*

We talked about how awe is a state we visit—we don't live in awe but journey into it, sometimes consciously and other times spontaneously. Having said that, we acknowledge that awe can become what you might think of as a normal part of life. By repeatedly resetting our nervous system, awe helps us shed unwanted sympathetic stress. The science shows that the more we bask in the wonder of awe, the more likely our brains will create connections and pathways on which our euphoria travels, triggering awe in response to an untold number of ordinary events.

Before getting into how awe becomes a way of life, we want to be certain you're intimately familiar with what awe feels like. If you've begun toying with the A.W.E. Method, you might have noticed that some experiences of awe feel more miraculous than others. Or you might be wondering whether you're in awe or feeling some other positive emotion, such as joy. Some of you might even be questioning whether this practice really works.

It's true that some of us are more prone to experiencing awe or feel it more intensely than others. We want to share why—and then explain that we really don't think it matters.

HOW DO YOU KNOW WHEN YOU'RE IN AWE?

Asking someone to describe awe is a bit like asking them to describe how air and sunshine feel. If we asked you to describe air or sunshine, your answer would depend on how much—or even whether—you pay attention to these elements. Some people don't even consider these things. Others notice and appreciate them but only peripherally. They might comment that it's a beautiful, sunny day, for instance. And still others deeply appreciate how the sun warms their skin, and they will take a moment or two to immerse themselves in the freshness of a spring-scented breeze. These sensations would repeat themselves even when the person recalls the experience. Yes, you can be in awe while experiencing sunshine and air as well as while remembering them.

Awe is felt on a spectrum ranging from subtle to energizing and what we call "awegasmic." When you practice A.W.E. and feel a shift—even if ever so slightly—to a more awakened state, you are feeling awe.

AWE SPECTRUM

Following are some words that might describe various "levels" of awe. You will likely come up with your own descriptors. But know that awe can be hard to define because the timelessness of Spacious Consciousness doesn't rely on words.

SUBTLE

pleasant, appreciative, joy, tender, satiated/satisfied, content, open/opening, connected, sweet, humility, well-being

EXPANSIVE

moved, captivated, connected, sweet, wonder/wondrous, vastness, flow state, energizing, astonished, slightly disoriented

AWEGASMIC

release of energy (goose bumps, shivers, chills), tingling, jaw dropping, ecstatic, connected to something greater than the self, reoriented, self-transcendent, radiant ecstasy, stupefied amazement, rapture, illumination, rhapsodic, ravished

An awe "awakening" may be soothing or stimulating. You may feel an increase in energy in your body or the release of energy. It's an individual experience that can vary depending on the object of awe and your context— are you alone or with other people, on task or relaxing, and are you starting from Safety or Heart Consciousness?

But why do some people feel awe more often or more intensely than others? And can we increase our propensity for feeling awe? There are several reasons why some people feel awe at the higher end of the spectrum. Some of it has to do with personality.

It's been nearly two years since learning about A.W.E. and Heart Consciousness, which overlap quite a bit in my practice. Before attending the A.W.E. course, I was certainly experiencing moments of awe and deep appreciation, though I lacked the language and framework to harness and expand it for me. When I practice awe now, the best description of how I change myself *is one that came from Jake—an uncoiling. When I am uncoiled, I tend to experience a softer ego—I have less need to correct others, interject, or gain attention around me. I also have an increased reception of the present, meaning I'm less concerned about scheduling or checking of time and more accepting of events as I encounter them. Lastly, I experience a worldly small- ness. Perhaps my favorite element of awe, this is when I see how small of a fleck of dust I am in this world, yet how precious a piece of dust that is.*[1]

—Tennison

BEING OPEN TO AWE

Ebenezer Scrooge and the Grinch have at least three things in common: they are fictional characters in best-selling books that have stood the test of time; they're introduced to readers as unhappy, ungrateful, closed-minded meanies; and through what we and others would describe as an "awe-based awakening"—for them, an epochal change in perspective—they blossom into grateful and compassionate beings.

We're not suggesting that if you never feel awegasmic you're a scrooge or a grinch. We use these examples to exaggerate a point: Certain personality traits have been shown to either lessen or enhance the awe experience. Yet we want to emphasize—and later in this chapter illustrate—that, as with our two fictional characters, regardless of your personality (some of which is inherited, by the way), repeatedly microdosing awe via A.W.E. expands your propensity to experience awe—even turning it from a state into a trait. Awe is an equal-opportunity emotion.

Awe is also a captivating, all-encompassing emotion. In a sense, it takes us over. Allowing such a powerful emotion "in" requires that we be *open* to the experience, which makes some of us feel too vulnerable, so we partially shut down.

Openness to experience is one of what's known as the Big Five personality traits. Though there are hundreds of personality traits, many psychologists believe that five core traits drive personality. In addition to openness, the Big

Five are conscientiousness, extroversion, agreeableness, and neuroticism.* None of these are either-or traits. They are measured on a continuum. And people you think of as open-minded or agreeable, for instance, can be stubborn and hardheaded in certain circumstances.

Of all the Big Five, openness is the one most associated with a greater capacity to experience awe. People who tend to be more open to new experiences might feel awe more strongly—the chills (goose bumps), the dropping jaw, the eyes wide open—than those who are less open to new experiences.[2]

In addition to openness, researchers have found that people who are wise and appreciative and who have little need for "cognitive closure," or a right or wrong answer, are more easily drawn to awe.[3] How much money you have in the bank can also play a surprising role. In a study on social class and awe, researchers concluded that people from a higher social class tended to experience "self-oriented" positive emotions such as pride and contentment, usually through personal achievements. Conversely, lower-income individuals were more likely to experience "other-oriented" emotions, such as love, compassion, and awe, around their relationships. What does income and class have to do with awe? The researchers surmised that the higher our social status, the bigger our ego, and the less open we are to awe's self-diminishing effects.[4]

Similarly, one paper that compared awe experiences among people from twenty-six countries found that the wealthier the nation, the more individualistic its citizens, and the more likely they were to credit themselves—instead of other people or situations—for their awe experience. Hitting a hole in one (United States; self-agency), for instance, compared to hearing a boy sing "Ave Maria" perfectly (Argentina; other-agency) versus witnessing the sunrise from the summit of Mount Fuji (Japan; situational).[5]

As far as we're concerned, awe knows no boundaries or limits. Regardless of your personality, using the A.W.E. Method repeatedly expands your propensity to elevate your awe experience. We refer to it as building your

---

* Personality develops through nature and nurture, but researchers estimate nearly half of our personality is inherited. What happens afterward depends on our environment—how safe and loved we feel, for instance.

A.W.E. muscle, and we'll explain how to do it later in this chapter. But we do acknowledge four aspects that truly *inhibit* awe, or make it less accessible: rigidity, dogma, excessive narcissism, and polarization. However, when people who suffer as a result of their own rigidity, dogma, narcissism, and polarization do experience awe, it can be even more powerful than it is for more open-minded people.

Kirk Schneider, author of *Awakening to Awe*, notes that accessing awe can be made more difficult if we've become numb to our feelings: "I have come to realize that the day I am immune to pain and am completely 'healed' is the day when I have become numb to life. Contrary to this, I believe that one cannot feel awe if one has not seen one's own wounds and accepted that scars are inevitable. For me, healing involves being in awe of my whole self, which requires great attention and appreciation of who I am, my shadow side not being an exception."[6]

Schneider's reference to the whole self—body, mind, and spirit—is an important one. Feeling the whole self means that we're in the present moment, wide open to what is. Our default mode network has been quelled. We're poised to fully embody awe, to allow our cells to marinate in it.

If we give ourselves the gift of awe—this whole-body experience—for at least five to fifteen seconds a few times a day, over time something remarkable happens: our brain begins to create new neural pathways to accommodate this sensation, laying down the wiring for future positive awe experiences.

FROM STATE TO TRAIT: THE CUMULATIVE EFFECT OF A.W.E.

Personality traits aren't set in stone from birth. They're somewhat malleable. We can become more agreeable or extroverted as we mature depending on our experiences. Like our identity, our personality can expand. This is partly because of the brain's quality of neuroplasticity, or its ability to learn and change through our experiences, which allows states to turn into traits.

States are, by definition, temporary and often, as with initial experiences of awe, fleeting. But what if we could select a state (hint, we're thinking of awe) and make it part of our personality? Scientists who study what happens in the brain during meditation are showing that we can do this.

When reviewing five studies that looked at meditation's effect on the brain, researchers found that a regular meditation practice changed the underlying neural circuitry in parts of the brain and thickened the gray matter in areas of the brain responsible for interoception, or our ability to describe how we feel.[7] Later, researchers from the University of North Carolina showed that repeatedly reaching a state of mindfulness over the course of an eight-week meditation class helped to turn the state of being mindful into a dispositional trait—part of the meditators' personality.[8]

One could argue that this is why mindfulness practices have been around for so long: when practiced regularly, they can hard-wire us into better people.

In *Neurodharma*, Rick Hanson describes specifically how we can hard-wire a state into the brain so that it becomes a trait. Key to this miracle of a feat is activating the state we wish to develop—in our case, feeling the emotion of awe. But, according to Hanson, there's one more step:

> I call the first stage *activation* and the second stage *installation*. This is *positive neuroplasticity*: turning passing states into lasting *traits*. The second stage is absolutely necessary. *Experiencing does not equal learning.* Without changing neural structure or function, there is no enduring mental change for the better.
>
> Most beneficial experiences pass through the brain like water through a sieve, leaving no value behind. You have a good conversation with a friend or feel calmer in meditation—and then an hour later, it could be like that never happened. If awakening is like a mountain, in some moments you may find yourself far up its slopes—but can you stay there, on firm footing? Or do you keep slipping back down again?[9]

A.W.E., as luck would have it, takes us through both steps. The activation stage requires having a beneficial experience, which occurs in the first part of

A.W.E. The installation stage requires absorbing the experience—reflecting on it briefly—and that occurs in the latter part of A.W.E.

As Rick Hanson says, "Traits are more reliable than states. You take them with you wherever you go. The problem is, most people have many good states that never become good traits. . . . Meanwhile, stressful, painful, harmful experiences are being rapidly converted into lasting changes in neural structure or function."[10] The A.W.E. Method is one way to take a good state and reinforce it.

The emotion of awe activates the learning process through cognitive accommodation and changes the neural structure of the brain. With neural pathways for awe set in place, the brain remembers the feeling. A.W.E. has a cumulative effect. The feeling of awe builds on itself over time so that the feeling (the state) turns into a trait and becomes part of who we are. As awe becomes part of our disposition, we become prone to experiencing spontaneous awe.

Practicing A.W.E. at least three times a day reinforces this brain activity—and rather quickly. In our UC Berkeley studies, some people reported feeling awe spontaneously after only three weeks. It's worth noting that most of our study participants had either never meditated before or had tried but given up.

For us, Jake and Michael, spontaneous awe moments have become a matter of course. After making a daily practice of taking in awe for a couple of years, Jake is convinced that he's rewired his brain. He acknowledges that is a strange thing to say, but there's no question that he's a happier, more resilient person than he was prior to this practice.

And after decades of a formal meditation practice, Michael now mostly practices A.W.E. After just a few months of using the A.W.E Method, he started experiencing spontaneous awe moments and no longer has to intentionally practice the method. Every aspect of his life is permeated with opportunities to spontaneously experience awe—while sitting at a red light, scrubbing in for surgery, or enjoying his morning cup of tea. The shifts have been both subtle and profound, with greater ease in all areas of his life, from intimate relationships to his career.

So whenever you feel awe, take it in for a few breaths and notice how it feels. Do this often and you will begin to experience the beauty of rewiring your brain for awe.

HOW ARE YOUR AWE NEURAL PATHWAYS DOING?

Has your A.W.E. muscle grown? Do you recall the awe survey we asked you to take in Chapter 1? If you've been practicing A.W.E., the frequency and intensity with which you experience awe has likely grown. Here's the survey again. Answer the questions to see whether your propensity for delighting in awe has increased.

DISPOSITIONAL POSITIVE EMOTIONS SCALE—AWE SUBSCALE

Rate how you feel about the statements that follow on a scale of 1 to 7, with 7 being the greatest:

I often feel awe.

I see beauty all around me.

I feel wonder almost every day.

I often look for patterns in the objects around me.

I have many opportunities to see the beauty of nature.

I seek out experiences that challenge my understanding of the world.

(continues)

(continued)

Tally up your points, which should range from 6 to 42. The higher your score, the more you naturally experience awe.

BUILDING YOUR A.W.E. MUSCLE

Now that you know how to do A.W.E. and experience awe as a state that you move in and out of, we want to help you develop awe into a trait—part of your character. Building your A.W.E. muscle leads to spontaneous awe, awe occurrences that take even less effort than the A.W.E. Method.

Although this book has presented a five- to fifteen-second process to enter the bliss of awe and Spacious Consciousness, we realize that some people benefit from a more structured approach to accessing awe. Anyone struggling to get beyond Safety or Heart Consciousness might consider making a twenty-one-day commitment to building the A.W.E. muscle. Twenty-one days may seem like an arbitrary number, but according to some researchers, it's the amount of time it generally takes to form a new habit. What should your first twenty-one days of awe look like? They can look like *anything you want*, but we've included a few ways to experiment with A.W.E. in different settings and situations, along with some tips that can help you commit to your goal of experiencing awe every day.

TWENTY-ONE DAYS OF A.W.E.

Following are some fun ways to start using A.W.E. We encourage you to journal about your A.W.E. experience; you can get a journal to write in or use your phone or a journaling app. Try to reduce your experience to one sentence. For example, here's one sentence that might capture your awe moment with a barista: "I see the same barista every day when I get my coffee, but today I noticed her beautiful smile."

WEEK ONE: DAYS 1–7

Nature

People seem to find awe most quickly and easily in nature. Even if you live in a crowded metropolis, you can usually find a piece of nature—a tree, hedge, bird, squirrel. For this week, each day, we invite you to pick one item in nature to explore deeply. For example, if you were to pick a tree, you could consider the following:

Its shape and its existence
The fact that a tree has roots
The tree's branches
A single leaf
An acorn or pine cone
The pollen that blows off the tree in the spring
A seedling that endures a strong wind

WEEK TWO: DAYS 8–15

In Your Environment

Awe is in the ordinary and so can be found wherever you are. This week, find awe in your living environment . . .

A book
A painting
Music
An heirloom
The silence
A clock
A meal

WEEK THREE: DAYS 16–21

In People

Relationships can be among our biggest joys as well as our greatest challenges. Try using A.W.E. when you're with or thinking about people—those you know well and those you've never met. How does awe affect how you feel about these people? Find awe in . . .

Someone you may not know well but you appreciate. This could be the clerk who checks out your groceries, a friendly neighbor, or a grateful client.

Someone you know well and love. A family member or friend, for instance. This person could be currently in your life in some capacity or no longer with you.

Someone you feel in conflict with, perhaps a family member you're reluctant to call for fear of instigating an argument. At the end of the week, after experiencing awe moments while thinking about this person, notice whether your attitude has changed. You might want to try this with people you think about often:

    A child who is acting out

    A disgruntled coworker

    A public figure you tend to disagree with

You can even try this exercise using yourself as the subject to create more self-love and compassion.

TIPS FOR DEVELOPING AN A.W.E. PRACTICE

Commit: Commit to practicing A.W.E. three to five times a day for twenty-one days. At first, you might want to set an alarm as a reminder. Before long, you will be doing it spontaneously—and often.

Begin: Begin with the Twenty-One Days of A.W.E. experiences. Then for one week practice A.W.E. with one of the experiments from Chapter 12 ("Sensorial Awe"). These are the experiments most people gravitate toward. For weeks 2 and 3, you might try the experiments in Chapters 13 and 14. Stick with the experiments you enjoy the most. And, of course, feel free to find your own awe moments.

Immerse Yourself: Be sure to relish your awe, hold the feeling for as long as you can. Really feel it for at least a couple of breaths. Feel it intensely to ensure that it becomes a hardwired, positive trait.

Share: A wonderful awe practice is to share your moments of awe and read about other people's moments of awe, which can be awe inducing in and of itself. We encourage you to post some of your awe experiences on the Moments of Awe page on our website (ThePowerOfAwe.com). You can use words or pictures to express your awe moments. The webpage holds moments of awe posted by members of our global Power of Awe Community. After a certain number of new moments are added, previous ones fade away, representing the temporary nature of all moments. Many people report experiencing awe moments from viewing other people's awe posts. We encourage you to visit the webpage and be inspired, even if you don't have an awe moment to share.

Journal: Journaling about your awe moments is helpful in several ways. It helps you embed your awe moments more deeply in your psyche and see the progress you're making. We encourage you to keep an awe journal and make entries whenever you can. Writing even a line or two is sufficient.

Buddy Up: Recruit an A.W.E. buddy to share your awe moments with. Talking about your experiences—whether spine-tingling awe moments or struggles to achieve them—can be revealing. We find that A.W.E. students enhance their experience by sharing awe moments, and you might be surprised by what you discover about yourself. These shares can be through email, text, in person, or over the phone, or in an online meeting. Your buddy doesn't need to be practicing A.W.E. They only need to be a good listener.

The purpose of this twenty-one-day commitment is not to criticize yourself or worry about whether you're doing the A.W.E. Method correctly. We as a society are used to trying hard to do something "right." But awe doesn't require force. Only presence.

If you were to visit the Grand Canyon, for instance, you probably wouldn't tell yourself in advance that you need to be in awe. Taking in the landscape would do the job. The beauty of A.W.E. is that we don't need to think about what we're doing; we only need to observe and let presence arise. Presence arises in the practice of A.W.E. when we're giving our full and undivided attention to things we value and appreciate. It's an all-encompassing experience that leaves no room for an agenda or judgment. Presence creates the space for the emotion of awe—and its accompanying "aha" moments—to enter.

> I still wear my "A.W.E." bracelet that I received when I went through the Power of Awe course, all the time, every day. I wear the bracelet because it reminds me several times a day, even if it's not overtly intentional, to stop for a few seconds and remind myself that life is still good. Despite the relentless bad news flooding our troubled world, my personal life is in reasonable order.[11]
>
> —Hari

AWE

Awe is everywhere. We don't need to travel to find it. There is no destination. We don't need to think about it. There is no analysis. We don't need to compare it. Each experience of awe is unique. Finding awe isn't a goal. Goals are for the future. Awe is here now, a sense of wonder coming from firsts, lasts, and experiences that continue to amaze us.

Firsts: First kiss. First love. First time you met your puppy. First time you were accepted into a program you wanted to join. First time you rode a bike, swam in the ocean, reached a peak.

Lasts: The last mountain you'll climb. Your last kiss. Last "I love you." Last caress. Last sip of water you'll drink. Last words you'll hear.

Experiences that continue to amaze: Sunrise. Shooting stars. Redwood trees. The Grand Canyon. Michelangelo's *David*. The Northern Lights. A sense of oneness. Andrea Bocelli's voice.

The depth of love we can feel.

The A.W.E. Method is a conduit for the vital gift of awe, a most powerful emotion that has the potential to polish every aspect of our emotional and spiritual life. With awe, the promise is not that life will be free of challenges or adversities. Rather, awe coats each moment with appreciation, gratitude, and presence, lending a richness, depth, and enlightened perspective to all life's ups and downs.

When we infuse our days with what brings us into Spacious Consciousness, we awaken from a slumber. We are no longer burdened by our past or worried about our future. We are no longer spiritual seekers. We no longer have to think about the A.W.E. process. It just happens. We delight ourselves with spontaneous and frequent experiences of awe. We revel in those moments. The effect is a profound peace and power of presence that leaves us deeply satisfied, even thrilled to be alive.

The next section offers more than thirty experiments to help you get started with your A.W.E. practice—or to enhance it. Just as each person's awe will always be unique to them—like snowflakes or fingerprints—each of us discovers awe differently.

PART V

DISCOVERING AWE

CREATED BY HANNAH EAGLE

People often say that "beauty is in the eye of the beholder," [but] I say that the most liberating thing about beauty is realizing that you are the beholder.

—*Salma Hayek*

We have designated three domains of awe: sensorial, interconnected, and conceptual. *Sensorial* awe arises when we allow ourselves to be fully present with our senses of sight, sound, scent, taste, and touch. *Interconnected* awe comes from having heart-opening experiences with other sentient beings. *Conceptual* awe arises when we imagine an idea or concept that expands our perspective, possibly to the point of being mind-boggling.

Each domain represents a different territory, and the experiments are meant to be road maps for exploring each territory. Because you may find it easier to access one domain over another, we encourage you to start with the experiments that feel most comfortable. Another option is to practice some bibliomancy and let this book fall open to any page in this final section and see what you discover.

Some of these experiments are examples of using the A.W.E. Method—they will only take five to fifteen seconds. Others are more like a journey. They will take a bit more time and offer multiple opportunities for you to experience *extended* moments of awe. We invite you to be curious as you go on these journeys—some will take you out in nature; others can be done in your home. All along the way, with each step you take, look for the awe.

CHAPTER 12

SENSORIAL AWE

Sensorial awe arises when we allow ourselves to be fully present with our senses of sight, sound, scent, taste, and touch. Experiments in this chapter encourage us to find awe in our immediate surroundings—while drinking our morning coffee, watching the clouds, or tending to our home or garden. Each experiment offers something for you to focus on as you use the A.W.E. Method.

CONNECTING WITH YOUR EYE-DENTITY

According to a new study by Yale University psychologists, most people intuitively feel as if their "self"—otherwise known as their soul, or ego—exists in or near their eyes.

—*Natalie Wolchover*

Begin by gazing at your eyes in the mirror. Get close enough to see your eyes clearly, not too close, but not too far. A magnifying mirror can enhance this experience.

Notice the variety of colors and lines and patterns and reflections of light.

According to an ancient art form, used across many cultures, your eyes will reveal your true character.

Look into your right eye. This is the eye that you show the world, your personality, your character. Who do you see?

Now focus on your left eye. This, they say, is your true eye. Look deeply. What's different about this eye? Here you can see your wisdom and your spirit and the imprint of your journey through life.

Look even deeper into that eye and ask who is in there looking back at you?

Can you see that you're looking out your eye—into the mirror—so as to look into your eye from the outside? Pretty wild!

SHOWERING

If your commitment is to being present, then there will come a time when being present becomes your natural state. The present moment becomes your home. You will have short excursions into the world of the mind, but you never go so far into the mind that you get lost there.

—Leonard Jacobson

Showering is an ordinary activity we do almost every day. It's a good place for creative thinking but also a great place for an awegasmic experience.

Slip into the stream gradually and notice the sensation of the water stimulating your arms, head, neck, face, back, and belly.

Turn around and around and stay with the sensation of water bouncing off your skin.

Play with different temperatures, hot to warm to cold and back to warm again.

Notice the sound of the water and the scents of soap and shampoo and the smooth soapy contact of your hands on your body.

The idea is to become impeccably aware and present to everything you are feeling and experiencing in this moment. Every step is an opportunity for awe.

When you feel complete, turn off the shower. Watch your arm as you reach for your towel. Notice the texture of the towel on your skin as it absorbs the water.

This is an awesome way to start your day: feeling lighter, more alive, even radiant.

What's next? Continue to move slowly and stay aware of this next moment.

WATCHING MOVEMENT

When was the last time you spent a quiet moment just doing nothing—
just sitting and looking at the sea, or watching the wind blowing the
tree limbs, or waves rippling on a pond, a flickering candle or children
playing in the park?

—Ralph Marston

On a day with a breeze, place yourself in a natural setting, a park, a shore-
line, or in the mountains.

Stand or sit quietly and begin to watch. Simply observe the movement of
trees, grasses, flowers, water, clouds, birds, insects, and people.

A whole visual and auditory orchestra is playing in the wind.

Begin to notice that everything has a rhythm. Every tree or blade of grass,
every cloud catches the breeze and moves in its own unique way.

As with nature, so are we . . . moving through the world in our own
special, individual ways. Unlike plants and clouds, we animals self-propel
ourselves, perhaps soothed by, but not propelled by, the breeze.

Over seven billion people on the earth, yet no one person moves like any
other.

THE MUSIC CONNECTION

Music gives a soul to the universe, wings to the mind, flight to the imagination, and life to everything.

—Plato

Music connects humans to other humans. And it's thought that we made music before we had language. Music connects us through rhythm, song, and dance and is expressed through culture as ritual and celebration.

When we hear or make music that we love, we release the happy hormones, dopamine and serotonin. These make us feel good.

When a piece of music you like catches your attention, listen to it in a deeper way than you ordinarily do. Connect yourself to the rhythm, the harmony, the pauses, and the crescendos. Notice each instrument or voice as it enters the score.

If you need an awesome suggestion, try "503"—Hans Zimmer with Joshua Bell.

Awe can be our delightful reward when we wake up and truly listen.

Close your eyes, listen, breathe it in, transport yourself. Give yourself wings.

BODY OF WATER

They both listened silently to the water, which to them was not just water, but the voice of life, the voice of Being, the voice of perpetual becoming.

—Hermann Hesse

Take your body of water (60 percent of your body is water) to a body of water—a lake, an ocean, a pond, a river, a fountain.

Still yourself. Notice any breeze and the warmth of the sun.

Notice sounds—ocean waves, rushing of the river, lapping of the lake shore, and the sound of wind moving through the leaves and the calling of birds.

Notice limbs swaying in the wind and then their swaying shadows on the ground.

Notice the many colors and patterns and reflections dancing on the surface of the water. Bright light reflecting off the water can energize you.

Touch the water; notice the sensations of cool and wet.

Allow yourself to really notice everything, not just to see.

TASTING

Listen to your life. See it for the fathomless mystery it is. In the bore-
dom and pain of it, no less than in the excitement and gladness: touch,
taste, smell your way to the holy and hidden heart of it, because in the
last analysis all moments are key moments, and life itself is grace.

—*Frederick Buechner*

Taste? How often do we fully taste a meal? When we eat, are we paying
attention? Immersing ourselves in taste sensations can be an awesome
experience.

How extraordinary is it that our taste buds can distinguish between
sweet, sour, salty, bitter, savory, tangy, spicy, and nuttiness!

Take something you love, something small: a raisin or nut, a piece of
chocolate, or a bite of banana.

Put a morsel in your mouth and experience first the temperature, then the
texture, then the taste.

Allow the flavor to fully saturate. Notice the desire to chew and also the
desire to swallow. Once you swallow, notice the desire, or not, for more.

Wait.

Then slowly taste the next morsel. Can you imagine being this present
during an entire meal, consciously tasting every bite? Try it.

Each little bit of a meal can induce a moment of awe when we're really
paying attention.

SUNSET

When your world moves too fast, and you lose yourself in the chaos, introduce yourself to each color of the sunset.

—*Christy Ann Martine*

Have you watched the sun slowly melt like butter into the horizon?

By witnessing the awe and beauty of the setting sun, you slow down your perception of time and stimulate hormones in your brain that will make you feel happy.

Find a place to watch the final moments of the setting sun. The colors slowly change before your eyes, from fiery reds and oranges to golden hues and deep violet.

Allow yourself to breathe in and out slowly and deeply. Let go of thoughts of the past and future, lose yourself in this colorful moment.

Every sunset is unique. So, this sunset will never be exactly like any other.

COOK LIKE A ZEN MONK

It was relaxing, silent and rhythmic. I got a chance to dive deep into the simple tasks of boiling water, sprinkling salt in, washing basil leaves, tearing fresh juicy mozzarella balls apart with my fingers, and chopping garlic. My mind had nothing to do other than the steps needed to make this happen. And in the end, there was the impulse to explore the beauty in colors contrasting each other on a plate when placed in specific places.

—*Food Practice*

The most envied job at any Zen center is that of the Tenzo, the cook. He or she gets to practice meditation in action for most of the day. You can be like a Tenzo today by giving the preparation of a meal *all* your attention.

Using your senses, notice your body moving across the kitchen to reach for things.

Notice the cold coming toward you when you open the refrigerator door and notice the heat you can feel from the stove.

Notice each movement that you make—the measuring and lifting, the pouring and stirring, and the color and aroma of each ingredient.

Consciously put one ingredient away before reaching for the next one.

Spoon your meal onto your plate as though it were a gift to yourself, which it is.

Sit quietly and eat consciously.

Attend fully to what you're doing at every step in the process while inhaling, waiting, and fully exhaling into awe.

ELEVATE YOUR GAZE

Eighty percent of the world's population does not lift its eyes above the horizon once a day.

—*Charles Darwin*

In preparing for an awe moment, take a walk in a park or the woods. Choose a quiet setting with a path that's fairly level and clear of any obstacles.

Begin walking slowly, focusing your attention on your feet with each step you take.

When feeling grounded, elevate your eyes so that your view is straight out in front of you rather than lowered toward the ground.

If thoughts arise, you'll likely find your gaze has gravitated toward the ground. If this happens, just notice and elevate your eyes again.

With elevated eyes, you are more present, and you feel far more alive and receptive to awe.

A SCENTSFULL CONNECTION

Smell is the primordial sense, more powerful, more primitive, more intimately tied to our memories and emotions than any other. A scent can trigger spiritual, emotional or physical peace and stimulate healing and wellness.

—Donna Karan

Have you ever deeply connected with the fragrance of things?

If flowers are blooming, you can begin searching for scents outside. But here's a scenting adventure you can have inside your house that will wake up your senses.

Start with your fragrant shower gel or shampoo. Take a moment to breathe in the scent, be it lavender or grapefruit or lemon or mint.

Really stay with the scent until you have fully connected with the fragrance, and then stay a little longer. Then move on to the next fragrance.

Toothpaste can smell like mint or cherries, sunscreen like coconut, even fragrance-free body lotion can have a subtle scent—one you might label "nourish me."

What a miraculous thing it is to have a nose that can connect with these fragrances, even the subtle ones. Some scents may even connect you with sweet memories.

ENHANCE THE DANCE

To dance is to be out of yourself. Larger, more beautiful, more powerful. This is power, it is glory on earth and it is yours for the taking.

—Agnes de Mille

Listening to music is a way to wake up our senses and make us feel more
alive. We can take in the music and let our body, rather than our mind, do
the moving.

Choose a song that you love.

Stand with closed eyes. Begin to breathe in the music.

Don't move, but first just feel the rhythm.

Then let the music move your body from the inside out.

Move, play, unwind, release, explore, improvise. Unleash yourself without caring what people think. No form to follow, let your body lead the way.

There'll be at least a few moments of awe as you free your body from your
mind.

BEING THE CENTER OF THE UNIVERSE

Whereas before the road, the sea, the trees, the air, the sun all spoke differently to me, now they spoke one language of unity. Tree took account of the road, which was aware of the air, which was mindful of sea, which shares things with sun. Every element lived in harmonious relation with its neighbor, and all was kith and kin. I knelt a mortal; I arose an immortal, I felt like that center of a small circle coinciding with the center of a much larger one.

—*Yann Martel*

Try this next time you're a passenger in a car on the open road and out away from city traffic.

While focusing straight ahead, without moving your eyes to the side, notice that you can expand your view to include the sides of the road.

While engaging this peripheral view, you can still see the road, but you can also experience the landscape passing by.

Begin to imagine that you and the car are standing still, and the road and landscape are moving past you.

For this awe moment, you can be the still center of a moving universe.

SLIDING INTO SLUMBER

Sleep is the best meditation.

—Dalai Lama

Before you get into bed, note how fortunate you are to have a comfortable bed to sleep on. This isn't true for everyone.

Wear as little as you're comfortable with so you have more skin contact with your sheets.

Notice your hands as they pull back the covers, exposing the sheets.

Slide yourself between the layers and sense the soft coolness as you move yourself inward to cocoon yourself for the night.

Take a deep breath, feel your body expand as you inhale deeply, and allow your whole body to sink into the bed, letting go of any tension in your face, your tongue, your jaw, your whole body as you exhale.

If you're really paying attention, this can be a moment of awe. Be grateful for these next hours of rest when you have not a thing to do.

CHAPTER 13

INTERCONNECTED AWE

Interconnected awe comes from having heart-opening experiences with other sentient beings. Such experiences can come from profound connections and companionship, witnessing, suffering, and acts of generosity, loss, and, most notably, love. You can use the A.W.E. Method to deeply connect with loved ones, pets, and even strangers.

CONNECTING WITH SOUNDS AND SILENCE

Listening is such a simple act. It requires us to be present, and that takes practice, but we don't have to do anything else. We don't have to advise, or coach, or sound wise. We just have to be willing to sit there and listen.

—*Margaret J. Wheatley*

Wherever you are, stop to listen to the sounds around you.

Then, notice the silence between the sounds.

Rest peacefully in this silence, relaxed and ready for the next sound.

In conversations, we can also connect in the silence between our shared thoughts.

These are moments to "be" together without trying to fill in the void.

And, if we practice connecting with one another in silence, these can be our most awesome and connected moments.

HUGS

You have to really hug the person you are hugging. You have to make the person very real in your arms. You don't do it just for the sake of appearance, patting the person on the back two or three times to pretend you are there. Instead, be really there, fully present. Breathe consciously while hugging, and hug with all your mind, body, and heart.

—Thich Nhat Hanh

We may share thousands of hugs over the course of our lives. Many are done on autopilot without noticing the hug at all. Build a moment of awe into a hug of your choosing. Just take those extra five to ten seconds to stop, pay attention, and consciously connect.

Notice how this body you're hugging feels as you hold them. As you breathe in, you may notice their warmth and their unique scent.

Stop thinking, just feel; wake up your senses. And when you or they are ready, let go.

Notice how remarkable a hug can be when you're fully aware and present for the connection.

CONNECTING WITH NATURE

There is a way that nature speaks, that land speaks. Most of the time we are simply not patient enough, quiet enough, to pay attention to the story.

—Linda Hogan

Find a place to sit in nature. Draw an imaginary six-foot circle around you.

Begin noticing what's inside your circle. Notice colors and textures and shadows and light.

Notice everything that is still, like stones and leaves and particles of earth. Perhaps each one of them has been waiting for eons to be noticed.

Next watch for movement, perhaps of ants and beetles and anything that flies.

Can you connect with these beings? Talk to them? You and they share this fleeting thing called life.

Imagine what it's like to be an ant or to be a bee. Like you, they breathe and feel and taste and hear, and they likely see you while you are seeing them.

The difference is that we humans can be conscious of the miracle of being alive if we only stop to notice.

CONNECTING WITH YOUR PET

Animals are the bridge between us and the beauty of all that is natural. They show us what's missing in our lives, and how to love ourselves more completely and unconditionally. They connect us back to who we are, and to the purpose of why we're here.

—Trisha McCagh

Our pets appreciate it when we slow down and give them our full attention.

Connecting with those we love—humans or animals—is one way to experience awe.

Lie down next to your beloved pet.

Slowly extend your hand or finger to their paw.

Fully take in this sweet moment and gentle connection.

Lie there for a while. Notice your breath.

Notice the pace of their breath compared to your own.

Be still for a moment with this unique and irreplaceable being.

CONNECTING WITH A STRANGER

Our best hope for the future is not to get people to think of all human-
ity as family—that's impossible. It lies, instead, in an appreciation of
the fact that, even if we don't empathize with distant strangers, their
lives have the same value as the lives of those we love.

—*Paul Bloom*

Standing in line can be experienced as an interruption in your day or as an
opportunity for a moment of awe. Next time you're standing in line, begin
to consider this as a gift of space and time in your busy life, and choose
gratitude.

Imagine breathing from your heart, take a deep breath, and begin to notice the scene around you.

Look around for strangers with whom you can connect, perhaps the person behind or in front of you.

For only a moment, allow yourself to have eye contact with this other human being—who's also been given the gift of time to stand in line.

MIRRORING

The beauty you see in me is a reflection of you.

—Rumi

Do this with a partner in silence. Stand face-to-face, palms lightly connecting with each other's palms. Choose who will be the mirror, and who will be the mover.

The mover begins by moving hands and arms, reaching out wide to the sides, in circles, and above their head. The mirror follows and reflects all the movement of the mover.

Begin moving at a comfortable pace, then when ready, slow down to slow motion. Notice how your sense of connection with your partner changes as your pace slows down. If you're very present, this is an opportunity for awe.

Now slow down further to make your movement almost imperceptible. And slowly settle into stillness, aware of your connection. Breathe in. Wait, exhale and expand with a smile.

TOUCHING HANDS

Sometimes, reaching out and taking someone's hand is the beginning of a journey. At other times, it is allowing another to take yours.

—*Vera Nazarian*

Sit quietly with a friend.

Reach out to gently hold their hands in your hands.

Breathe deeply. Notice warmth and coolness and a felt sense of connection.

Begin to explore these hands, lightly touching every hill and valley and every line. These hands hold a story. They contain impressions from their life lived so far and perhaps forecasts of their future.

In these hands are remnants of hopes and dreams, regrets and sorrows, loves and losses, and hopefully millions of delightful moments.

The cells in these hands are genetically connected to the first humans on earth and contain elements of stardust from billions of years ago. They are a continuation of all that has come before them.

Now, offer your hands to your friend, to begin a journey of their own.

UNIQUE SIGNATURE

Today you are You, that is truer than true. There is no one alive who is Youer than You.

—Dr. Seuss

Everyone is as unique as their fingerprints. Each person moves through life in their own special way.

When you're in the presence of someone you know well, pay attention to whatever shines thorough as unique to them. Notice how they drink their tea or coffee, or how they walk or talk, or their special way of laughing.

Allow yourself to focus on and appreciate whatever is memorable, captivating, or endearing about them and experience awe in this completely unique being before you.

There is no one alive who is them-er than them.

NOTICING ESSENCE

No one can become fully aware of the very essence of another human being unless he loves him.

—Viktor E. Frankl

When you find yourself with a person or pet who is sleeping, stop, take a moment to notice this unique and quiescent being.

You are seeing them now without the distraction of personality. There's no discernable movement happening, nor words nor behavior nor activity to define them.

There is only their quiet essence resting in this moment in time. Notice what you appreciate. Notice what you love.

This can easily be a moment of awe.

CONNECTING WITH A FRIEND

All other spiritual teachings are in vain if we cannot love. Even the most exalted states and the most exceptional spiritual accomplishments are unimportant if we cannot be happy in the most basic and ordinary ways, if, with our hearts, we cannot touch one another and the life we have been given.

—Jack Kornfield

Find a friend who wants to share a moment of awe.

Sit back-to-back and gently touch your head to their head. Close your eyes.

Begin breathing deeply. Try to relax and connect with the sensation of breathing. Soften and sink into the moment.

Then begin to synchronize your breathing with your friend's.

Breathe in, expand your chest, making greater space for your heart, then send your exhale and your love into your friend. On your inhale, receive the love from them.

EYE CONTACT

If we are to love our neighbors, before doing anything else we must see our neighbors. With our imagination as well as our eyes, that is to say like artists, we must see not just their faces but the life behind and within their faces. Here it is love that is the frame we see them in.

—*Frederick Buechner*

Gaze into the eyes of a friend or a loved one.

Take time to notice, not just to look.

Imagine the history of this person, all the loves and losses, joys and disappointments, fears and accomplishments, written on their face and reflected in their eyes.

Inhale deeply, open your heart, understand and love them for who they are and all they might like to be.

HOLDING HANDS

Last night I woke up with someone squeezing my hand. It was my other hand.

—William S. Burroughs

The next time you reach for someone's hand, whether for a handshake or to walk together, hand in hand, do this more consciously.

Notice your desire to connect first. Then focus on your hand as it extends toward the other person.

Upon making contact, notice the warmth or coolness of their skin, the pressure you feel from their grip, whether strong or gentle, and the emotion you feel while making this connection.

Being totally present for this small, ordinary activity can give rise to a moment of awe.

CHAPTER 14

CONCEPTUAL AWE

Conceptual awe arises when we imagine an idea or concept that expands our perspective, possibly to the point of being mind-boggling. Here, we're asked to look for the miracle in the many aspects of life we tend to take for granted—the miracle of the body, being alive, water, memory, invention—and to explore sweeping concepts such as the constancy of change, death and dying, spaciousness, and changing perspective.

SPACE

If you want to make an apple pie from scratch, you must first invent the universe.

—Carl Sagan

Take a human hair.

The width of that hair is around a million atoms across.

And atoms aren't just tiny, they are 99.9 percent empty space.

If you removed all the empty space from the atoms that make up all the humans on the planet, you could fit all of us, every human on the planet, inside a single apple.

TAKING TIME

It's being here now that's important. There's no past and there's no future. Time is a very misleading thing. All there is ever, is the now. We can gain experience from the past, but we can't relive it; and we can hope for the future, but we don't know if there is one.

—George Harrison

Look at the time. This is the only moment in all recorded and unrecorded history or in the future, for that matter, that this second in this minute of this hour on this day will happen.

Stop. Look around, pay attention, open your senses. Don't miss *this* moment in time.

In a fraction of a second, this moment will be gone forever. Whoops, it's gone . . . how about this one?

GRAVITY

In his eyes shone the reflection of the most beautiful planet in the Universe: A planet that is not too hot and not too cold; that has liquid water on the surface and where the gravity is just right for human beings and the atmosphere is perfect for them to breathe; where there are mountains and deserts and oceans and islands and forests and trees and birds and plants and animals and insects and people—lots and lots of people. Where there is life. Some of it, possibly, intelligent.

—Stephen Hawking

Unless you're feeling an earthquake, you won't feel the earth move under your feet—even though the earth is spinning at the speed of a thousand miles per hour and orbits the sun at a speed of about sixty-seven thousand miles per hour.

How is it that we aren't having to hold on for dear life and why don't we feel the movement? Gravity is the answer; the fact that, like riding in a car, we're on board, going for the earth ride.

The great mass of the earth and the weight of our bodies create a gravitational attraction toward each other. The heavier we are, the stronger the force of gravity, and thus the harder it is to jump away from the earth into the air.

We weigh something because we connect with the earth, and yet, the earth weighs nothing because it's in free fall as it orbits the sun.

THE GIFT OF WATER

We really have the most beautiful planet in our solar system. None other can sustain life like we know it. None other has blue water and white clouds covering colorful landmasses filled with thriving, beautiful, living things like human beings.

—*Sunita Williams, astronaut*

Pour yourself a glass of water. Give this clear, life-sustaining liquid your full attention. Take a sip and swallow. Notice the sensation of water sliding down your throat. Then contemplate these remarkable facts about the water we drink:

There is an estimated 326 million trillion gallons of water on Earth.

Much of this water originally came from comets and asteroids.

In a hundred years, a water molecule spends ninety-eight years in the ocean, twenty months as ice, about two weeks in lakes and rivers, and less than a week in the atmosphere providing the water you drink through rainfall.

The amount of water on this planet, now, is the same as when the earth was formed. So, there could be molecules in the water you're drinking that a dinosaur drank sixty-six million years ago!

WATCHING CLOUDS

This morning after yoga, I laid in the grass and watched the white clouds go by as the earth turned slowly, and it was the single most beautiful thing, that I started to cry.

—Erika B.

Have you ever stopped long enough to watch clouds move through the sky?

And what is a cloud anyway?

The word *cloud* comes from Old English and refers to a lump of water in the sky. Which is just what it is, and a heavy lump at that. A cloud is composed of small water droplets or ice crystals.

The average cumulus cloud weighs over a million pounds. A million floating pounds. And a big thunderstorm can weigh over a billion pounds.

Imagine this: there is a water vapor cloud in outer space that holds one hundred trillion times the amount of water on the entire surface of the earth.

THE AWE OF NOTHING

If Life could speak, being still is listening closely to what it has to say. . . . Being still awakens us to the lessons embedded inside every single creation that is right in front of us, just waiting to be noticed.

—Ethel M. Do

Physicists gathered in 2013 to discuss whether such a thing as "nothing" exists. They agreed that empty space with nothing in it was not nothing and that a dark, empty space is still something.

One physicist argued that there is a deeper kind of nothing that consists of no space at all, and no time, no particles, no fields, no laws of nature.

Contemplation is a deeper kind of nothing, but doing nothing is still something we "do." If doing nothing was simply "being" quiet and still, with an empty mind, and not thinking—just being entirely present—would we be doing nothing?

Try to "be" still and "do" nothing. That space between thoughts can be quite something.

RAINBOWS

In a perfect world, human beings would co-exist harmoniously, like a rainbow. A multitude of colors, each layer vibrant and clear by itself, but in unison, boundless, breathtaking, celestial.

—Mariah Carey

Imagine driving down the highway and suddenly the pavement turns to mud. Your car will likely skid, slow down, and change direction. That is what happens when a wave of sunlight hits a raindrop. It slows and changes direction.

These skidding waves of light in the raindrop then bounce out to form the rainbow colors, lining up in the same order every time—red on top, violet on the bottom, and all other colors in between.

If there is a double rainbow, the colors in the second one line up in the opposite order.

A rainbow is really a circle, not just an arc, though we can see only the top half. If we observed the rainbow from an airplane, or the top of a tall mountain, we would see the full circle.

There is even something rare called a moonbow, a rainbow at night from refracted moonlight that can be witnessed (seen) in only seven places on Earth.

We can only see the rainbow if the sun is behind and the rain in front of us, and no two people will ever see the same rainbow.

So, you are the only being in the universe who will ever see the rainbow you see.

THIS HUMAN BODY

Every single cell in the human body replaces itself over a period of seven years. That means there's not even the smallest part of you now that was part of you seven years ago.

—Steven Hall

Turn your hands palms up. Look for a vein in your wrist. Take note that if you stretched out the blood vessels in your body and laid them end to end, the length would almost circle the earth three times.

Now, take a deep breath, filling your lungs with air, and imagine this:

If we measured the surface area of your lung, it would be equal to the size of a tennis court.

If we stretched out your small intestine, it would be about twenty-three feet long.

If we consider the average of one hundred thousand hairs on your human head, and we measured the length all your hairs together will grow over your lifetime, it would be about 450 miles long.

If we counted the number of times your heart will beat by the age of seventy, it will have beaten an average 2.5 billion times.

There are trillions of cells in your awesome human body, and each cell has a brain of its own that's called DNA, and each of those cells holds a complete story of the universe and the history and future of everybody.

CONNECTING WITH THE STARS

Look up at the stars and not down at your feet. Try to make sense of what you see and wonder about what makes the universe exist. Be curious.

—*Stephen Hawking*

On a clear, starry night, take a blanket outside, preferably somewhere with less light pollution, and lie down on your back.

Close your eyes for a moment. Breathe deeply.

Open your eyes and focus on a bright star. Then expand your vision, without moving your eyes, to include the entire sky.

You're looking at the vastness of one single galaxy, our own galaxy, the Milky Way, consisting of over a billion stars. Since the beginning of human history this is what people saw on every cloudless night.

We know there are at least a hundred galaxies out there beyond this one. The universe is infinitely big and has no edge. The galaxy you see and all galaxies beyond are constantly expanding outward and will likely expand in space forever.

This means that, since the Big Bang, the planets and stars are still moving away from one another. Like raisins in a rising loaf of bread, the space around them expands, and like the stars, the raisins get farther and farther apart.

Breathe in the vastness, wait, exhale and expand yourself out with the stars.

You might feel small and big at the same time and connected to everything.

WHERE ARE YOU?

Everybody has a little bit of the sun and moon in them. Everybody has a little bit of man, woman, and animal in them. Darks and lights in them. Everyone is part of a connected cosmic system. Part earth and sea, wind and fire, with some salt and dust swimming in them. We have a universe within ourselves that mimics the universe outside.

—*Suzy Kassem*

You're sitting on a planet in the middle of nowhere.
    Spinning at about a thousand miles per hour.
    Floating in empty space that has no beginning or end.
    Where will you be tomorrow?
    Sitting on a planet in the middle of nowhere.
    Spinning at about a thousand miles per hour.
    Floating in empty space that has no beginning or end.

EPILOGUE

The Future of A.W.E.

W e started this book by confessing that we were almost embarrassed when we found a shortcut to transcendence. But like the shortcuts we rely on when using a computer keyboard, A.W.E. is a sequence of neurological and physiological keys that elevate consciousness, improve relationships, and accelerate healing, well-being, and personal growth—a shortcut worth taking.

When practiced enough, A.W.E. has a cumulative effect, and soon we begin to experience spontaneous awe moments when we least expect them. This is more than delightful. It's powerful. A.W.E. has the potential to change us.

We feel these changes as pronounced shifts—in our health and well-being, responses, attitude, approach to people and situations—indicating that our brain cells are establishing new pathways. These shifts indicate that we're turning the typically fleeting state of awe into a trait—a part of who we are as a person.

But the A.W.E. Method is more than a self-help technique, and the implications of awe go well beyond personal transformation. Awe touches everything, and perhaps most telling is the effect it has on others. We're wired to attune to others' behaviors and moods; our nervous system senses the emotions of those around us. Just as being the recipient of a warm smile can lighten our mood, when we're in awe, those around us feel it too. Awe is contagious. And so, practicing the A.W.E. Method is one not-so-small way we can contribute to the world.

In this book, we covered how the A.W.E. Method is grounded in science and that a whole body of science supports that awe changes lives. So, we have a big cymbal-crash ending to the power behind the simple practice of the A.W.E. Method: If practiced frequently enough by enough people—a critical mass, as it were—everyone would experience a significant, heightened shift in consciousness.

Awe changes us and when we share our awe, we change the world.

How can we be in awe of someone and physically or emotionally harm them?

How can we be in awe of the natural world and destroy it?

How can we be in awe of life itself and not live as if every day were a miracle?

In awe, the tone of every conversation—from the personal to the political—shifts from having an agenda to being open and curious. Our conversations impact how we raise our kids, how we help our aging parents, how we treat our spouse, how we participate in community, how we mentor or supervise people, how we govern a city, and how we lead a nation.

We can think of no downside to practicing the A.W.E. Method because awe is the light—the appreciation of nature and different cultures, the curious and open mind, the generous and giving soul—even during times of darkness. These days, we need awe more than ever.

Awe awaits you—and surrounds you—in the ordinary moments of your life. Like the view of the stars that fill the night sky, awe is free and available. All you need to do is pay attention to what you value, appreciate, and find amazing—wait—and then exhale and expand into the unlimited, timelessness of awe.

ACKNOWLEDGMENTS

First and foremost, we want to thank our cowriter and researcher Karen Chernyaev for helping us discover and tell the story of awe. Her skill, perseverance, and faith in the process contributed significantly to making us proud of this book. Karen immersed herself fully in this project, joining one of our twenty-one-day awe courses so that she had firsthand experience. She continued to practice as we all worked together to write this book. It became personal for her, and we hope she benefited from working with us as much as we benefited from working with her.

From the first day of this project, Hannah Eagle was our partner in discovering A.W.E. and creating practical awe exercises to help us and our readers experience awe in the ordinary. She is gifted at taking concepts and showing people how to embody them—turning mental constructs into felt senses, which makes the experience more personal, powerful, and sustainable.

Without Dacher Keltner's enthusiastic support and guidance our research would not have taken place. Dacher recognized the significance of our A.W.E. methodology before we did, believing it could be used as a medical intervention. Not only is Dacher one of the foremost experts on awe, but he cares deeply about finding ways to introduce people to awe so that they fly. He gave us wings and we are forever grateful.

Our literary agent at Park & Fine Literary Agency, Jaidree Braddix, has guided us through this process with sharp insights and aloha spirit. The team at Hachette Publishing includes our editor Renée Sedliar, who is smart, funny, and insightful, as well as Mary Ann Naples, publisher; Michelle Aielli, associate publisher; Michael Barrs, marketing director; Sharon Kunz, publicist; Quinn Fariel, marketing manager; Sean Moreau, senior production editor and project manager; Amy Quinn, production coordinator and designer; Terri Sirma, cover designer; Christina Palaia, copyeditor; Lori J. Lewis and Annie Chatham, proofreaders; and Robie Grant, indexer.

Felicia Zerwas, Rebecca Corona, Ozge Ugurlu, and Maria Monroy were the graduate students at UC Berkeley who worked tirelessly to help us design and conduct the UC Berkeley/NorthBay Hospital studies. They supported us and the study participants during the studies, and then crunched all the data to produce our evidence-based papers that capture and convey our results.

Rick Hanson, Kirk Schneider, and Judson Brewer—experts in their own fields—generously spent time with us helping us deepen our understanding of mindfulness, awe, and neuroscience.

We are grateful to David Hanscom, MD, for welcoming us to the weekly Dynamic Healing Discussion Zoom calls he has been orchestrating for the past two years. The focus of the group is for doctors, researchers, scientists, psychologists, and academics to share ideas for improving our health-care system and finding new ways to deal with chronic disease. The group relies on the innovative theory of Stephen Porges, the creator of the polyvagal theory. In addition to David and Stephen, we appreciate the meaningful guidance offered by all the members, especially Sue Carter, Tor Wager, Howard Schubiner, Alan Gordon, D. R. Clawson, and Les Aria.

Along the way, we have benefited from the guidance and generosity of many people. Thank you—Katharine Rivers, Mike Bundrant, Shauna Shapiro, members of the Live Conscious community, participants in the UCB/NorthBay Awe Study, Deb Dana, Canton Becker, Olivia Seay, Aylana Zanville, and members of the meditation group Michael founded in Davis, California.

Both of us, like most innovators, are harvesting the fruits of seeds that were planted by other people. For Jake, my primary mentors were John and Joyce Weir, and Nelson Zink. Without their generosity, the harvest would not be nearly as bountiful. For Michael, my mentors at Spirit Rock Meditation Center, specifically Rick Hanson, Rabbi Greg Wolf, Rick Foster, and Roger Walsh, have inspired and supported me on my journey. These are just a few of the many mentors who guided me on a long journey as a physician and a mindfulness teacher.

Finally, I, Jake, want to thank Michael Amster for partnering with me on this project, drawing me out of semiretirement to do something that feels significant at this stage in my life. This book is a chance to share psychological models and practical tools that Hannah and I inherited from our mentors, as well as others that we developed, culminating in the development of A.W.E. It was Michael's ability to open doors, connect with the right people, and make things happen in what seemed like moments instead of months that brought this project to fruition. As a result of working together, the tools in this book are available to more people, and it is my hope that these tools will reduce emotional suffering while helping people elevate their consciousness, conversations, and spirit. Thank you, Michael.

And I, Michael, want to acknowledge my mentor of sixteen years, Jake. It is my hope that this project will introduce more people to some of your, and Hannah's, innovative, inspiring, and pragmatic ways to help people fulfill their potential. The years of work you did before we started on this project provide a foundation and framework that help us understand why awe is such a powerful emotion, as well as helping us understand when, where, and with whom to exercise our awe muscle. I've come to understand what you're all about is helping people reach their potential. Thank you for helping me get closer to reaching mine.

NOTES

INTRODUCTION: A SHORTCUT TO TRANSCENDENCE

1. Dacher Keltner and Jonathan Haidt, "Approaching Awe, a Moral, Spiritual, and Aesthetic Emotion," *Cognition and Emotion* 17 (2003): 297–314.

CHAPTER 1: THE SCIENCE OF A.W.E.

1. Sarah Mervosh, Denise Lu, and Vanessa Swales, "See Which States and Cities Have Told Residents to Stay at Home," *New York Times*, updated April 20, 2020, https://www.nytimes.com/interactive/2020/us/coronavirusstay-at-home-order.html.

2. Michael Daly, Angelina R. Sutin, and Eric Robinson, "Longitudinal Changes in Mental Health and the COVID-19 Pandemic: Evidence from the UK Household Longitudinal Study," *Psychological Medicine* (November 2020): 1–10, https://doi.org/10.1017/S0033291720004432.

3. Paul K. Piff and Jake P. Moskowitz, "Wealth, Poverty, and Happiness: Social Class Is Differentially Associated with Positive Emotions," *Emotion* 18, no. 6 (2018): 902–905, https://doi.org/10.1037/emo0000387.

4. Marshiari M., survey response to authors, October 25, 2021.

5. Angela (alias), email to authors, January 5, 2022.

6. Michelle N. Shiota, Dacher Keltner, and Oliver P. John, "Positive Emotion Dispositions Differentially Associated with Big Five Personality and Attachment Style," *Journal of Positive Psychology* 1, no. 2 (2006): 61–71, https://doi.org/10.1080/17439760500510833.

7. Denise (alias), email to authors, February 22, 2022.

8. Saloni Dattani, Hannah Ritchie, and Max Roser, "Mental Health," Our World Data, published April 2018, last modified August 2021, https://ourworldindata.org/mental-health; Syed Mustafa Ali Shah et al., "Prevalence, Psychological Responses and Associated Correlates of Depression, Anxiety, and Stress in a Global Population, During the Coronavirus Disease (COVID-19) Pandemic," *Community Mental Health Journal* (October 27, 2020): 1–10, https://doi.org/10.1007/s10597-020-00728-y.

9. Debra J. Brody and Qiuping Gu, "Antidepressant Use Among Adults: United States, 2015–2018," NCHS Data Brief No. 377, September 2020, https://www.cdc.gov/nchs/products/databriefs/db377.htm.

10. Omar A. Almohammed et al., "Antidepressants and Health-Related Quality of Life (HRQoL) for Patients with Depression: Analysis of the Medical Expenditure Panel Survey from the United States," *PLoS One* 17, no. 4 (April 20, 2022), https://doi:org/10.1371/journal.pone.0265928.

11. Clara Strauss et al., "Mindfulness-Based Interventions for People Diagnosed with a Current Episode of an Anxiety of Depressive Disorder: A Meta-Analysis of Randomized Controlled Trials," *PLoS One* 9, no. 4 (April 24, 2014): e96110, https://doi.org/10.1371/journal.pone.0096110; Robyn Della Franca and Benjamin Milbourn, "A Meta-Analysis of Mindfulness Based Interventions (MBIs) Show that MBIs Are Effective in Reducing Acute Symptoms of Depression but Not Anxiety," *Australian Occupational Therapy Journal* 62, no. 2 (April 2015): 147–148, https://doi.org/10.1111/1440-1630.12198.

12. Jacob Piet and Esben Hougaard, "The Effect of Mindfulness-Based Cognitive Therapy for Prevention of Relapse in Recurrent Major Depressive Disorder: A Systematic Review and Meta-Analysis," *Clinical Psychology Review* 6 (August 31, 2011): 1032–1040, http://doi.org/10.1016/j.cpr.2011.05.002.

13. Natalie (alias), email to authors, February 23, 2022.

14. Alice Chirico and Andrea Gaggioli, "The Potential Role of Awe for Depression: Reassembling the Puzzle," *Frontiers in Psychology*, April 26, 2021, https://doi.org/10.3389/fpsyg.2021.617715.

15. Andrea Gaggioli, email message to Michael Amster, October 19, 2021.

16. Natalie M. Golaszewski et al., "Evaluation of Social Isolation, Loneliness, and Cardiovascular Disease Among Older Women in the US," *JAMA Network Open* 5, no. 2 (February 2, 2022): e2146461, http://doi.org/jamanetworkopen.2021.46461.

17. Julianne Holt-Lunstad, Timothy B. Smith, and J. Bradley Layton, "Social Relationships and Mortality Risk: A Meta-Analytic Review," *PLoS Medicine*, July 27, 2010, https://doi.org/10.1371/journal.pmed.1000316.

18. Jacob Sweet, "The Loneliness Pandemic," *Harvard Magazine*, January–February 2021, https://www.harvardmagazine.com/2021/01/feature-the-loneliness-pandemic.

19. Yang Bai et al., "Awe, the Diminished Self, and Collective Engagement: Universals and Cultural Variations in the Small Self," *Journal of Personality and Social Psychology* 113, no. 2 (May 2017), https://doi.org/10.1037/pspa0000087; Patty Van Cappellen and Vassilis Saroglou, "Awe Activates Religious and Spiritual Feelings and Behavioral Intentions," *Psychology of Religion and Spirituality* 4, no. 3 (2012): 223–236, https://doi.org/10.1037/a0025986.

20. Jayaram Thimmapuram et al., "Heartfulness Meditation Improves Loneliness and Sleep in Physicians and Advance Practice Providers During COVID-19 Pandemic," *Hospital Practice* 49, no. 3 (August 2021): 194–202, http://doi.org/10.1080/21548331.2021.1896858.

21. Estelle (alias), email to authors, November 2, 2022.

22. Christopher Cheney, "Expert: Healthcare Worker Burnout Trending in Alarming Direction," Healthleaders, December 15, 2021, https://www.healthleadersmedia.com/clinical-care/expert-healthcare-worker-burnout-trending-alarming-direction; "The Mental Health Impact of COVID-19 Pandemic on U.S. Healthcare Workers, First-Responders,"

News Medical Life Sciences, last reviewed December 16, 2021, https://www.news-medical
.net/news/20211216/The-mental-health-impact-of-COVID-19-pandemic-on-US-health
care-workers-first-responders.aspx; Anupam Das et al., "A Study to Evaluate Depression
and Perceived Stress Among Frontline Indian Doctors Combating the COVID-19 Pandemic," *Primary Care Companion for CNS Disorders* 22, no. 5 (October 8, 2020), http://
doi.org/10.4088/PCC.20m02716; Sara Berg, "Half of Health Workers Report Burnout
Amid COVID-19," American Medical Association, July 20, 2021, https://www.ama-assn
.org/practice-management/physician-health/half-health-workers-report-burnout-amid
-covid-19.

23. Kriti Prasad et al., "Prevalence and Correlates of Stress and Burnout Among U.S.
Healthcare Workers During the COVID-19 Pandemic: A National Cross-Sectional Survey Study," *eClinicalMedicine*, May 16, 2021, http://doi.org/10.1016/j.eclinm.2021
.100879.

24. "The Mental Health Impact of COVID-19 Pandemic on U.S. Healthcare Workers, First-Responders," News Medical Life Sciences, last reviewed December 16, 2021,
https://www.news-medical.net/news/20211216/The-mental-health-impact-of-COVID-19
-pandemic-on-US-healthcare-workers-first-responders.aspx.

25. Thomas L. Rodziewicz, Benjamin Houseman, and John E. Hipskind, "Medical Error
Reduction and Prevention," *StatPearls* (Treasure Island, FL: StatPearls Publishing, January
4, 2022), https://tinyurl.com/4abx4yzn.

26. Molly C. Kalmoe, Matthew B. Chapman, Jessica A. Gold, and Andrea M. Gieding-
hagen, "Physician Suicide: A Call to Action," *Missouri Medicine* 116, no. 3 (2019): 211–216,
https://www.ncbi.nlm.nih.gov/pmc/articles/PMC6690303/.

27. Kathleen Bartholomew, "The Dauntless Nurse: Had Enough Yet? The Latest on
Nurse Burnout," *American Nurse*, April 8, 2021, https://www.myamericannurse.com
/my-nurse-influencers-the-dauntless-nurse-nurse-burnout/.

28. Christopher Cheney, "Expert: Healthcare Worker Burnout Trending in Alarming Direction," Healthleaders, December 15, 2021, https://www.healthleadersmedia.com
/clinical-care/expert-healthcare-worker-burnout-trending-alarming-direction.

29. Maslach Burnout Inventory, https://www.psychosomatik.com/wp-content
/uploads/2020/03/Maslach-burnout-inventory-english.pdf.

30. Ben Wigert and Sangeeta Agrawal, "Employee Burnout, Part 1: The 5 Main Causes,"
Gallup, July 12, 2018, https://www.gallup.com/workplace/237059/employee-burnout-part
-main-causes.aspx.

31. Lara Pinho et al., "The Use of Mental Health Promotion Strategies by Nurses to
Reduce Anxiety, Stress, and Depression During the COVID-19 Outbreak: A Prospective
Cohort Study," *Environmental Research* 195 (April 2021): 110828, http://doi.org/10.1016/j
.envres.2021.110828.

32. Juliana Kaplan and Andy Kiersz, "2021 Was the Year of the Quit: For 7 Months,
Millions of Workers Have Been Leaving," *Insider*, December 8, 2021, https://www
.businessinsider.com/how-many-why-workers-quit-jobs-this-year-great-resignation
-2021-12; Jay L. Zagorsky, "Are We Really Facing a Resignation Crisis?" World Economic Forum, January 13, 2022, https://www.weforum.org/agenda/2022/01/great
-resignation-crisis-quit-rates-perspective/.

33. Paul Piff and Dacher Keltner, "Why Do We Experience Awe?" *New York Times*, May 22, 2015, https://www.nytimes.com/2015/05/24/opinion/sunday/why-do-we-experience-awe.html.

34. "Stress in America 2020: A National Mental Health Crisis," American Psychological Association, October 2020, https://www.apa.org/news/press/releases/stress/2020/report-october.

35. Craig L. Anderson, Maria Monroy, and Dacher Keltner, "Awe in Nature Heals: Evidence from Military Veterans, At-Risk Youth, and College Students," *Emotion* 18, no. 8 (2018): 1195–1202, https://doi.org/10.1037/emo0000442.

36. Melanie Rudd, Kathleen D. Vohs, and Jennifer Aaker, "Awe Expands People's Perception of Time, Alters Decision Making, and Enhances Well-Being," *Psychological Science*, August 10, 2012, https://doi.org/10.1177/0956797612438731; Amie M. Gordon et al., "The Dark Side of the Sublime: Distinguishing a Threat-Based Variant of Awe," *Journal of Personality and Social Psychology* 113, no. 2 (2017): 310–328, https://doi.org/10.1037/pspp0000120.

37. Jennifer E. Stellar et al., "Positive Affect and Markers of Inflammation: Discrete Positive Emotions Predict Lower Levels of Inflammatory Cytokines," *Emotion* 15, no. 2 (April 15, 2015): 129–133, https://doi.org/10.1037/emo0000033.

38. Sally (alias), email to authors, January 18, 2022.

39. James Dahlhamer, Jacqueline Lucas, Carla Zelaya, Richard Nahin, Sean Mackey, Lynn DeBar, Robert Kerns, et al., "Prevalence of Chronic Pain and High-Impact Chronic Pain Among Adults—United States, 2016," *Morbidity and Mortality Weekly Report*, September 14, 2018, https://www.cdc.gov/mmwr/volumes/67/wr/mm6736a2.htm.

40. John E. Sarno, *Healing Back Pain: The Mind-Body Connection* (New York: Grand Central Publishing, 1991), 32.

41. Alan Gordon with Alon Ziv, *The Way Out: A Revolutionary, Scientifically Proven Approach to Healing Chronic Pain* (New York: Penguin Random House, 2021), 28.

42. Marianne C. Reddan and Tor D. Wager, "Brain Systems at the Intersection of Chronic Pain and Self-Regulation," *Neuroscience Letters* 702 (May 29, 2019): 24–33, http://doi.org/10.1016/j.neulet.2018.11.047.

43. Rebecca (alias), email to Michael Amster, November 12, 2021.

CHAPTER 2: THE SCIENCE OF HEALING

1. Roma Pahwa, Amandeep Goyal, and Ishwarlal Jialal, "Chronic Inflammation," *StatPearls* (Treasure Island, FL: StatPearls Publishing, September 28, 2021), https://tinyurl.com/3sj4hkj2.

2. David Roger Clawson et al., "Post Covid-19 Syndrome: Threat versus Safety Physiology" (unpublished paper, July 26, 2021): https://backincontrol.com/wp-content/uploads/2022/07/Post-Covid-19-Syndrome-7.29.22.pdf.

3. Sally S. Dickerson et al., "Social-Evaluative Threat and Proinflammatory Cytokine Regulation: An Experimental Laboratory Investigation," *Psychological Science* 20, no. 10 (2009): 1237–1244, https://doi.org/10.1111/j.1467-9280.2009.02437.x.

4. David Roger Clawson, Zoom interview with authors, March 22, 2022.

5. Clawson et al., "Post Covid-19 Syndrome."

6. Jennifer E. Stellar et al., "Positive Affect and Markers of Inflammation: Discrete Positive Emotions Predict Lower Levels of Inflammatory Cytokines," *Emotion* 15, no. 2 (April 15, 2015): 129–133, https://doi.org/10.1037/emo0000033.

7. Neal Kearney, email to Michael Amster, April 22, 2022.

CHAPTER 3: UNVEILING AWE

1. Kimberlee D'Ardenne, "Research That Takes Your Breath Away: The Impact of Awe," *ASU News*, January 3, 2019, https://news.asu.edu/20190103-research-takes-your-breath-away-impact-awe.

2. Dacher Keltner, Zoom interview with authors, November 24, 2021.

3. Summer Allen, "Eight Reasons Why Awe Makes Your Life Better," *Greater Good Magazine*, September 26, 2018, https://greatergood.berkeley.edu/article/item/eight_reasons_why_awe_makes_your_life_better; Grace N. Rivera et al., "Awe and Meaning: Elucidating Complex Effects of Awe Experiences on Meaning in Life," *European Journal of Social Psychology* 50, no. 2 (2019): 392–405, https://doi.org/10.1002/ejsp.2604.

4. Kirk Schneider, interview with authors, December 24, 2021.

5. Ryota Takano and Michio Nomura, "Neural Representations of Awe: Distinguishing Common and Distinct Neural Mechanisms," *Emotion* 22, no. 4 (2022): 669–677, http://dx.doi.org/10.1037/emo0000771.

6. Dacher Keltner, Zoom interview with authors, November 24, 2021.

7. John Muir, *Nature Writings: The Story of My Boyhood and Youth, My First Summer in the Sierra, the Mountains of California, Stickeen, Essays* (New York: Penguin Putnam, 1997), 139.

8. D. M. Stancato and Dacher Keltner, "Awe, Ideological Conviction, and Perceptions of Ideological Opponents," *Emotion* 21, no. 1 (August 12, 2019): 61–72, http://dx.doi.org/10.1037/emo0000665.

9. Libin Jiang et al., "Awe Weakens the Desire for Money," *Journal of Pacific Rim Psychology* (January 1, 2018), https://doi.org/10.1017/prp.2017.27.

10. Melanie Rudd, Kathleen D. Vohs, and Jennifer Aaker, "Awe Expands People's Perception of Time, Alters Decision Making, and Enhances Well-Being," *Psychological Science* 23, no. 10 (August 10, 2012): 1130–1136, https://doi.org/10.1177/0956797612438731.

11. Rutger Bregman, *Humankind: A Hopeful History* (New York: Little, Brown, 2020), 118.

12. Bregman, *Humankind*, 110.

13. Duke University, "Oxytocin Enhances Spirituality: The Biology of Awe," *ScienceDaily*, September 21, 2016, https://www.sciencedaily.com/releases/2016/09/160921085458.htm.

14. Bregman, *Humankind*, 122.

15. V. E. Sturm et al., "Big Smile, Small Self: Awe Walks Promote Prosocial Positive Emotions in Older Adults," *Emotion*, September 21, 2020, Advance online publication, http://dx.doi.org/10.1037/emo0000876.

16. Bethany E. Kok et al., "How Positive Emotions Build Physical Health: Perceived Positive Social Connections Account for the Upward Spiral Between Positive Emotions and Vagal Tone," *Psychological Science* 24, no. 7 (July 1, 2013): 1123–1132, https://doi.org/10.1177/0956797612470827.

17. J. Holt-Lunstad, T. B. Smith, and J. B. Layton, "Social Relationships and Mortality Risk: A Meta-Analytic Review," *PLoS Med* 7, no. 7 (2010): e1000316, https://www.doi.org/10.1371/journal.pmed.1000316.

CHAPTER 4: *A*—ATTENTION: RENDERING OUR REALITY

1. William James, "Chapter XI. Attention," in *The Principles of Psychology* (1890), Classics in the History of Psychology, https://psychclassics.yorku.ca/James/Principles/prin11.htm.

2. Jenny Odell, *How to Do Nothing: Resisting the Attention Economy* (Brooklyn, NY: Melville House, 2019), 120.

3. James, "Chapter XI. Attention."

4. Jason Silva, "Awe," YouTube video, 2:48, May 23, 2013, https://www.youtube.com/watch?v=8QyVZrV3d3o&t=2s.

5. HeartMath, "The Science of HeartMath," https://www.heartmath.com/science/.

CHAPTER 5: *W*—WAIT: BECOMING PRESENT

1. Marcus Raichle, "What Your Brain Does When You're Doing Nothing," YouTube video, 5:55, January 9, 2019, https://www.youtube.com/watch?v=0r15-Xde66s.

2. ScienceDirect, Default Mode Network page, https://www.sciencedirect.com/topics/neuroscience/default-mode-network.

3. Michael Pollan, *How to Change Your Mind* (New York: Penguin Books, 2018), 260.

4. Tor Wager, email to Jake Eagle, July 26, 2021.

5. Tor Wager, email to Jake Eagle, July 26, 2021.

6. Jennifer M. Mitchell, Dawn Weinstein, Taylor Vega, and Andrew S. Kayser, "Dopamine, Time Perception, and Future Time Perspective," *Psychopharmacology* 235, no. 10 (October 2018): 2783–2793, https://doi.org/10.1007/s00213-018-4971-z.

CHAPTER 6: *E*—EXHALE AND EXPAND: FINDING
YOUR NERVOUS SYSTEM'S SWEET SPOT

1. Stephen Porges, email to Jake Eagle, September 1, 2021.

2. Stephen Porges, "Vagal Pathways: Portals to Compassion," in *Oxford Handbook of Compassion Science*, ed. Emma M. Seppälä et al. (New York: Oxford University Press, 2017), 192.

3. Jennifer (alias), email to authors, October 23, 2021.

4. Kelly Bulkeley, *The Wondering Brain* (Oxfordshire, UK: Routledge, 2004), 4.

5. Anil Seth, "Your Brain Hallucinates Your Conscious Reality," TED2017, 16:52, April 2017, https://www.ted.com/talks/anil_seth_your_brain_hallucinates_your_conscious_reality/up-next?language=en.

6. Seth, "Your Brain Hallucinates Your Conscious Reality."

7. Tija Ragelienė, "Links of Adolescents Identity Development and Relationship with Peers: A Systematic Literature Review," *Journal of the Canadian Academy of Child and Adolescent Psychiatry* 25, no. 2 (Spring 2016): 97–105, https://www.ncbi.nlm.nih.gov/pmc/articles/PMC4879949/.

8. Michael Pollan, "Dissolving the Default Mode Network" (interview with Simulation: Global Enlightenment), YouTube video, 6:27, June 14, 2018, https://www.youtube.com /watch?v=c71BY2RzZjY.

CHAPTER 7: WHAT IS MINDFULNESS, ANYWAY?

1. Tainya C. Clarke et al., "Use of Yoga, Meditation, and Chiropractors Among U.S. Adults Aged 19 and Over," NCHS Data Brief No. 325, November 2018, https://www.cdc .gov/nchs/products/databriefs/db325.htm.

2. Edward Bonner and Harris Friedman, "A Conceptual Clarification of the Experience of Awe: An Interpretative Phenomenological Analysis," *Humanistic Psychologist* 39, no. 3 (July 2011): 222–235, https://doi.org/10.1080/08873267.2011.593372.

3. Kirk Schneider, Zoom interview with authors, December 24, 2021.

4. Willoughby B. Britton, "Can Mindfulness Be Too Much of a Good Thing? The Value of a Middle Way," *Current Opinion in Psychology* 28 (August 2019): 159–165, https://doi .org/10.1016/j.copsyc.2018.12.011.

5. Rick Hanson, Zoom interview with authors, February 1, 2022.

6. Jennifer (alias), email to authors, October 23, 2021.

CHAPTER 8: HOW SPUTNIK LAUNCHED A NEW TREATMENT FOR ANXIETY

1. Tim Folger, "Does the Universe Exist If We're Not Looking?" *Discover*, June 1, 2002, https://www.discovermagazine.com/the-sciences/does-the-universe-exist-if-were -not-looking.

2. Folger, "Does the Universe Exist If We're Not Looking?"

3. Folger, "Does the Universe Exist If We're Not Looking?"

4. Pat Croce, *Lead or Get Off the Pot!: The Seven Secrets of a Self-Made Leader* (New York: Fireside, 2004), xiii–xiv.

5. Ginger (alias), email to Jake Eagle, March 22, 2022.

6. Philip J. Mix, "A Monumental Legacy: The Unique and Unheralded Contributions of John and Joyce Weir to the Human Development Field," *Journal of Applied Behavioral Science* 42, no. 3 (September 2006): 276–299.

7. Walt (alias), email to Jake Eagle, March 22, 2022.

8. Carl Rogers, *Carl Rogers on Encounter Groups* (New York: Harper & Row, 1970), 11.

CHAPTER 9: THE THREE LEVELS OF CONSCIOUSNESS

1. Erin (alias), email to Jake Eagle, November 10, 2021.

2. Trevor (alias), email to Jake Eagle, October 31, 2021.

CHAPTER 10: FINDING AWE IN TIMES OF STRIFE

1. Viktor E. Frankl, *Man's Search for Meaning* (Boston: Beacon Press, 2014), 37.

2. Carlo Rovelli, *The Order of Time* (New York: Riverhead Books, 2018), 121.

3. Summer Allen, "The Science of Awe" (white paper for the John Templeton Foundation, Greater Good Science Center, UC Berkeley, September 2018), 35–36, https://ggsc .berkeley.edu/images/uploads/GGSC-JTF_White_Paper-Awe_FINAL.pdf.

4. Tom (alias), email to authors, February 3, 2022.

5. Phyllis Norris, phone interview with Michael Amster, November 6, 2021.

6. J. E. Stellar et al., "Awe and Humility," *Journal of Personality and Social Psychology* 114, no. 2 (2017): 258–269, https://doi.org/10.1037/pspi0000109.

7. Kyla Rankin, Sara E. Andrews, and Kate Sweeny, "Awe-full Uncertainty: Easing Discomfort During Waiting Periods," *Journal of Positive Psychology* 15, no. 3 (September 18, 2018): 338–347, https://doi.org/10.1080/17439760.2019.1615106.

8. Y. Joye and J. W. Bolderdijk, "An Exploratory Study into the Effects of Extraordinary Nature on Emotions, Mood, and Prosociality," *Frontiers in Psychology* 5 (October 2015), https:// doi.org/10.3389/fpsyg.2014.01577.

9. Cheryl (alias), email to Michael Amster, November 12, 2021.

10. Kirk J. Schneider, "Standing in Awe: The Cosmic Dimensions of Effective Psychotherapy," *The Psychotherapy Patient* 11, nos. 3–4 (2001): 123–127.

11. Kirk Schneider, *Awakening to Awe: Personal Stories of Profound Transformation* (Lanham, MD: Jason Aronson, 2009), 79.

12. E. P. Courtney, J. L. Goldenberg, and P. Boyd, "The Contagion of Mortality: A Terror Management Health Model for Pandemics," *British Journal of Social Psychology* 59, no. 3 (2020): 607–617, https://doi.org/10.1111/bjso.12392.

13. Iva, email to Jake Eagle, February 21, 2021.

14. Neal Krause and R. David Hayward, "Assessing Whether Practical Wisdom and Awe of God Are Associated with Life Satisfaction," *Psychology of Religion and Spirituality* 7, no. 1 (2015): 51–59, http://dx.doi.org/10.1037/a0037694.

CHAPTER 11: TWENTY-ONE DAYS OF A.W.E.

1. Tennison (alias), email to authors, December 5, 2021.

2. Summer Allen, "The Science of Awe" (white paper for the John Templeton Foundation, Greater Good Science Center, UC Berkeley, September 2018), 21–22, https://ggsc .berkeley.edu/images/uploads/GGSC-JTF_White_Paper-Awe_FINAL.pdf.

3. Allen, "The Science of Awe," 21–22.

4. Paul K. Piff and Jake P. Moskowitz, "Wealth, Poverty, and Happiness: Social Class Is Differentially Associated with Positive Emotions," *Emotion* 18, no. 6 (2018): 902–905, https://doi.org/10.1037/emo0000387.

5. Enna Yuxuan Chen, "Cultural Variations in the Appraisals of Awe" (BA thesis, UC Berkeley, April 2020), https://escholarship.org/content/qt0dh4s9j3/qt0dh4s9j3_no Splash_96ce18233db1b4eed319ae43f3bf341a.pdf?t=qdxe5m.

6. Kirk Schneider, *Awakening to Awe: Personal Stories of Profound Transformation* (Lanham, MD: Jason Aronson, 2009), 86.

7. Ulrich Ott, Britta Hölzel, and Dieter Vaitl, "Brain Structure and Meditation: How Spiritual Practice Shapes the Brain," in *Neuroscience, Consciousness and Spirituality. Studies in Neuroscience, Consciousness and Spirituality*, vol. 1, ed. H. Walach, S. Schmidt, and W. Jonas (Dordrecht: Springer, 2011), https://doi.org/10.1007/978-94-007-2079-4_9 .

8. Laura G. Kiken et al., "From a State to a Trait: Trajectories of State Mindfulness in Meditation During Intervention Predict Changes in Trait Mindfulness," *Personality and Individual Differences* 81 (July 2015): 41–46, https://doi.org/10.1016/j.paid.2014.12 .044.

9. Rick Hanson, *Neurodharma* (New York: Harmony Books, Random House, 2020), 126.

10. Rick Hanson, "Growing Inner Resources for a Challenging World" (slide presentation, ITRC Building Human Resilience for Climate Change meeting, November 3, 2016), slides 20–24, https://tinyurl.com/2p8wnrjj.

11. Hari (alias), email to authors, March 22, 2022.

INDEX

ABOUT THE AUTHORS

Photo courtesy of Anna Pacheco

Jake Eagle, LPC, is a psychotherapist, mindfulness instructor, and author. For more than thirty years, Jake has innovated novel approaches to psychotherapy, helping people create meaningful lives and healthy relationships by emphasizing maturity, presence, and intentional states of consciousness. He is passionate about helping others fulfill their potential. In 2003, he and his wife, Hannah, cofounded Live Conscious, an organization offering on-line courses and life-changing retreats at awe-inspiring locations around the world. In addition to *The Power of Awe*, Jake is the author of two books. His first book, *Live a Conscious Life* (formerly titled *Speak Love Not War*), won the Independent Publisher Book Award.

Jake lives with Hannah in Hawaii—writing, researching, mentoring, and experiencing awe every day.

Photo courtesy of Carly Pence © ImCarlitohPhoto

Michael Amster, MD, is a physician and faculty member at Touro School of Medicine. He graduated from the University of California Irvine School of Medicine and completed his pain management fellowship at the University of Iowa. As a student of meditation for more than thirty years, as well as a certified yoga teacher and meditation teacher trained at Spirit Rock Meditation Center, Michael has taught spine health yoga classes and founded a Buddhist sangha/interfaith meditation group, which he led for seven years and occasionally returns to as a visiting teacher. Michael has been working as a pain management specialist for nearly twenty years and is currently the director of the pain management services at Santa Cruz Community Health, where he splits his time between clinical work, research on awe, teaching mindfulness, and leading awe-inspiring retreats around the world.

For more information, visit ThePowerOfAwe.com, Jake and Michael's website, which has a list of their upcoming retreats and workshops, online course, online community, and free content, including the Moments of Awe page.